Hope Rea

Tuscan artists; their thought and work, with notes on other schools

Principally for the use of travellers. Second Edition

Hope Rea

Tuscan artists; their thought and work, with notes on other schools
Principally for the use of travellers. Second Edition

ISBN/EAN: 9783337207441

Printed in Europe, USA, Canada, Australia, Japan

Cover: Foto ©Paul-Georg Meister /pixelio.de

More available books at **www.hansebooks.com**

TUSCAN ARTISTS

Their Thought and Work

With Notes on Other Schools

Principally for the Use of Travellers

By HOPE REA

WITH INTRODUCTION BY

SIR W. B. RICHMOND, K.C.B., R.A.
SOMETIME SLADE PROFESSOR AT THE
UNIVERSITY OF OXFORD

WITH 31 PLATES

SECOND EDITION

LONDON
GEORGE REDWAY
1898

All rights reserved

INTRODUCTION

THE closing years of this century are not proving themselves remarkable for imagination in matters that relate to Art, either literary or plastic. It is full of signs of change, whether for better or no who shall say? The temperament of the critic seems to be directed in a destructive, rather than a constructive spirit. The old order is changing, no doubt; but there are still sensitive, receptive, and cultivated minds that regard with respect, ay, with love, simpler moments in the history of the development of the mind, when men were guided by higher, if stronger and more violent feelings.

These included a passionate love for beauty, and an ardent regard towards religion, which, while they hold a part in our lives, in the lives of the Greeks and the Italians through many generations were paramount.

Emotions were ennobled by Christianity in various

directions; those in regard to beauty were enlarged but not changed, modified but not crushed.

Christianity preached love; Paganism gave to the world the outer beauty—they both revealed an inward calm. Both are offsprings of Divine law—brothers, indeed, that have never been completely divorced, either in fact or in sympathy.

Love and beauty were united by the great artists and artificers of Greece and Italy—from Kalamis to Pheidias, from Giotto to M. Angelo—who enriched the inheritance of future and countless ages by planting everywhere their immortal conceptions, to the service of the State, of humanity, and of religion.

In consequence of the hurry of life, so evidently becoming a part of the modern system, and the distractions and thoughtlessness inseparably its adjuncts, are induced apathy or cynicism.

Perhaps travellers of to-day are brought face to face with the great Art of the past as others never were. They see much. Perchance too quickly, too superficially! The majority return to their homes unenlightened as they left them, and it may be a matter for question if to their minds has been added one beautiful impression received and thought out to a final issue.

INTRODUCTION

Slower travel and deeper insight would enable intelligent travellers to verify the various chapters of this little book, and maybe to become enthusiasts as is its author.

Enjoyment, to be complete, must combine the senses and the intellect—in the nature of things a rare combination.

To have enjoyed a work of art to the full implies that the æsthetic sense has been satisfied in conjunction with the faculties of reason.

It is by patience, by prolonged study of a few works of art, either literary, plastic, or musical, that the whole nature is satisfied.

Because the great masters of design, the originators, have been few, whilst the many of ability have followed in their wake.

This idea has been well worked out in the second and third chapters. Those which deal with Donatello, Ghirlandaio, Raphael, and Michael Angelo, have been curtailed by necessity, for the subject is a very large one, and could not have been treated with anything approaching exhaustion in short essay.

The value of the book remains, in that the author has covered a large field of history, and by no means superficially; she does not advance a theory without the supplement of an argument in favour of noble motives.

I desire success for this little volume, so interesting, so full of sympathy with those various emotions whose expression in all forms of Art has made Italy their foster-mother.

W. B. RICHMOND.

4th June 1898.

The Author wishes to thank Messrs. Alinari of Florence and Naya of Venice, for kind permission to reproduce a number of their photographs.

TABLE OF CONTENTS

CHAPTER I

PAGE

The influences which determined the character of Building in North and Central Italy; and the influence of the Goldsmith instinct and training on Tuscan Art—Sandro Botticelli considered as representative Tuscan artist 11

CHAPTER II

The relation between Imagination and Reality in Art—In Tuscan Art, Fra Angelico considered as idealist; Luca Signorelli, in his work at Orvieto, as realist . 45

CHAPTER III

The fusion of these two influences, as seen in certain aspects of the work of Raphael, and the manner of their manifestation in the Art of Venice . . . 72

CHAPTER IV

The mediæval artist united with his own functions those of the printer—Popular stories (sacred and classic) being frequent subjects of architectural decoration—Giotto, Duccio, Carpaccio, and Raphael in this connection 100

TABLE OF CONTENTS

CHAPTER V

Originality of subject not considered by Italian artist —Tradition determined subject, originality lay in treatment—The development of treatment of various subjects traced—Allegory in Mediæval Art—Contrast between pictorial and sculptural treatment of same subject 133

APPENDIX

Thought scheme, and details of Orcagna's Tabernacle of Or San Michele — Early Florentine memorial slabs 174

TUSCAN ARTISTS

CHAPTER I

BUILDERS AND GOLDSMITHS

THE days when the art of Italy might be a delight only to the few who could afford the luxury of the grand tour are now for ever over. Each year increases the number of those who are able to visit Italy, or at least enjoy the growing riches of our own National Gallery and South Kensington Museum, which at length have begun to open their doors on the one day in the week when the People have leisure to visit their own in these treasure-houses.

To many, however, when the attention is once turned to the subject of Italian art, with any appreciation and spirit of inquiry, it must, in this first view, appear a field bewilderingly wide in its extent, and foreign in its nature. Looking with modern eyes at this art of a past age, it cannot but be felt that in style and method, and in its conception of things, it is an art that by no possibility could be produced to-day among ourselves; and yet that in its own day and country it must have been the outcome of the thought of normal men, working for a public which demanded and accepted their work, becomes obvious if the matter is considered seriously at all. How else indeed could any national art come into existence?

For the specialist and the amateur there exists a tremendous literature treating of the subject in its every aspect; but this, for the ordinary traveller or visitor to our home galleries, by reason of its very volume, is perhaps even more bewildering than the art itself. But if, without labouring through sections of this great art literature, the hurried person could yet come to understand, in some measure, how and why these older artists thought thus and thus, and not otherwise, how and why their art took the forms it did, and not such as those to which our artists aim to-day, it might surely be reckoned some advantage. At least, a step would be taken towards having passing curiosity transformed into intelligent interest, and a certain basis would be laid for the enjoyment of this great art from which it would be possible, if inclination prompted, to pass on to further study, and as a consequence, to further and profounder pleasure. A knowledge of names and dates and schools, and other matters more purely artistic, might follow, and if so, would fall naturally into their respective places, because, an intelligent foundation having been laid, the

BUILDERS AND GOLDSMITHS

art to which all these relate will have become alive —no longer a dead thing of museums and ancient churches, but the product of the glowing thought of actual men whose genius and age prompted them to give such and such form to their thought, and whom we feel to be, and to live behind their art.

In the following pages is an attempt thus to present the Italian Mediæval and Renaissance artists, their Work and their Thought, that the former may appear a natural outcome of the latter, and the men themselves living persons, the natural outcome of the traditional, historical, social, and religious conditions of their time, even as we ourselves are of the corresponding conditions of our time.

In such an attempt as that just proposed, naturally it is to Architecture that we must first turn, since Building is the foundation of all great art. The nomadic shepherd and huntsman may be a smith, and work sword-hilts with delicacy, and set them with jewels; he may weave and dye fabrics in varied colours, and touch with art the utensils needed for domestic use; but the fresco, the sculptured frieze, or the statue are to him, a tent or a hut dweller, obvious impossibilities. Architecture is necessarily the mother of the great arts in Italy as elsewhere.

But when the Italian architects arose after the dark days of the barbarian invasions in the early centuries of our era, and began again to build, they already started from a certain vantage-ground. They were not compelled to go to the beginning and learn the first steps of building; they had not to invent methods, and design forms as necessity demanded, without any background of tradition to help them, as was the case with earlier schools of building, and to a certain extent even with our later Northern Gothic architects. In Italy, before these newer Italian builders, there had been Rome—Rome itself, the Imperial City, and, besides, all the provincial towns taking Rome for their pattern. Nearly every mediæval Italian city had been Roman once, informed with Roman art, and with the tradition of that art stamped into the very soil. Though Byzantium had been made the seat of the Empire,[1] and to enrich the new capital, Rome had been robbed of innumerable treasures of art; though what Constantine left the barbarians treated with ignorant violence, and the Christianised Italians with scornful neglect, yet of building, pure and simple, much was left, from end to end of the peninsula. So the re-awakened Italians, in their turn, had not to invent and discover so much as to revive what had once been familiar knowledge.

Now one great feature at once marks the departure of architecture from the primitive to the scientific, and that is the presence and use of the *Arch*. In the Greek temple the arch is absent. Exquisite though it may be from the point of view of art, constructively the

---

[1] Constantine removed the capital of the Empire from Rome to Byzantium in 330 A.D.

Greek temple is primitive. Based on the lintel instead of the arch, virtually the construction has not advanced far beyond that of Stonehenge,—two uprights and a crossbar are its prime elements. And though treated never so beautifully, such building is building under primitive limitations; always must the space spanned be limited by the cohesive power of the lintel, and always must the height and consequent weight above, be limited by the bearing power of the lintel. But once let the arch be introduced, and architecture is set free. The space which may be spanned is practically unlimited; with nicely calculated balance, counterbalance, thrust, and support, any height may be obtained, any form secured, any material used; arch building is truly building at liberty. A mental comparison of the Parthenon, with its level lines and contracted form, all held together only so far as its lintels have the power to hold, with any Northern Gothic church—Salisbury, York, or Amiens—will at once bring out and demonstrate the virtue of the arch in building, and the possibilities which it creates.

Unlike the Greeks, the Romans had a knowledge of the arch, so that architectural form it was not necessary for the Italian Builders to discover. The Coliseum in Rome, the Amphitheatre in Verona, still in part remain, and show us with what freedom and skill the Roman architect could and did bring the arch into use. These, in more perfect condition than at present, and numberless other ancient monuments, remained to show the early Italians how to build; and with objects such as these before them, it is obvious what would and did become their attitude of mind with regard to building. They turned in their present ignorance respectfully to the past for enlightenment and teaching. In classic tradition they found their architectural ideal.

At first, like children, they spoiled the things they loved by over-much handling, with results curious enough to the eye of the northern traveller. A church in the little city of Lucca, dedicated to San Frediano—an early Irish missionary much revered throughout Tuscany—is an excellent instance of the methods of the early Italian builder. (Illustration 1).

On entering this church, one is struck by a strong contrast between its plan as a whole, and the treatment of its detail. Constructively, it is very simple. The nave is supported by an arcade, the arches of which have plain squared edges, with no ornamental mouldings whatever, and the walls are equally unadorned. Evidently the pride and joy of the whole building are the columns which support the arcade; these give the church its chief beauty. But these columns, held together, as some are, with bands of iron, look centuries older than, and vastly different in style from, the church; and so indeed they are. Carved with skill and delicacy, never could they have been the work of the masons who turned the arches now above them, and left those arches without any

Plate I.

SAN FREDIANO. INTERIOR.
From a photograph by Alinari.

To face page 16.

further touch of decoration. With one or two exceptions, the columns, with their carved Corinthian capitals, are veritable antique work, from the hands of some Roman sculptor of the Imperial age. Where they came from, who can tell us now with certainty? But somewhere, presumably near old Lucca, they must have been, at one time, fronting a pagan temple, or supporting the roof of a basilica. Appreciating the delicate beauty of this ancient sculpture, and knowing at the same time their own inability to work the like themselves, the seventh-century Lucchese builders in their admiration brought them to adorn their new church, built in honour of the beloved Frediano; and out of their very admiration, completed the demolition of the classic building, which time or the barbarians had probably begun.

And this church is but a typical instance of the methods of the early Italian builder; San Frediano is one of scores. Sometimes we may see columns of various lengths employed thus, and the springing of the arch brought down to meet the shorter stature of the cherished specimen of antique work—any device rather than not employ it. Again, sometimes may be seen even a part of an antique capital surmounting a column, and the necessary length made up by an additional piece of marble, dressed by the church's actual mason, as far as he was able to do so, into a crude imitation of the older work. In the church of San Miniato al Monte, near Florence, are one or two such instances, clearly indicating the attitude of the early Italian towards the work of the great age which preceded him.

But to return to San Frediano. It may also serve as a typical example of an old Italian church in the matter of ground plan and elevation. A nave and side aisles, separated from each other by a colonnade, and terminated by a rounded end or apse, is the usual form. Small windows occur above the colonnade, but no triforium, while the ceiling is of wood, sometimes open to the timbers, but more generally flat. The altar is on the chord of the apse, and the stalls for the clergy are *behind* the altar, not in front of it, as with us, but ranged around the wall of the apse.

This form and arrangement is extremely simple, sometimes even bald, to the northern eye, accustomed to the varied and complicated effects of Gothic building. But the peculiar richness of Northern Gothic must not be looked for in Italy : that was the outcome of another race, with other needs and aspirations in building, and less hampered by venerable traditions. The Italian was always in part Roman, and in the planning of his church, we see he followed closely after the pattern of the Roman Basilica, or public hall and law court. The Basilica style clings even to this day to the Italian mind. But, though so simple constructively, it is capable of a rich and stately dignity. No one could enter any of the great Basilicas in Rome, Santa Maria Maggiore, or San

BUILDERS AND GOLDSMITHS

Giovanni Laterano, for example, or the smaller San Pietro di Cassinensi in Perugia, without being profoundly impressed. The simple lines of the construction lend themselves to a splendid style of decoration which gives the whole an imperial effect.

But while dead Rome exerted such a strong influence on the Italian builder, Byzantium, the still living head of the Eastern Empire, had also a share in forming and modifying his taste. Byzantium had developed an art all her own, and purely Christian. In architecture she differed very much from Rome. The ground plan of the Byzantine church was in the form of a Greek cross, and the whole was surmounted by a cupola. Symbolism rather than tradition led the Byzantine builder, and he looked forward instead of backward in his art—hence the greater originality of his work. On the eastern coast of Italy, the influence of Byzantium was strongly felt, and Greek artists were largely employed there as builders, bronze-casters, and workers in mosaic. Ancona and Ravenna were even politically of the Greek Empire, and at Venice, though politically independent, arose the exquisite church of San Marco, as Byzantine as Byzantium itself. It is cruciform in plan, has a central dome, besides cupolas at the end of each arm of the cross, while the interior is encrusted throughout with marbles and mosaics entirely in the Byzantine manner.

Reference has been made above to the barbarian

invasions from which the Italian peninsula suffered in the early Christian centuries. Not all, however, of these peoples were mere ravagers and spoilers. Among them were the Lombards, who, appearing towards the close of the sixth century, made a permanent settlement in the land. When they finally identified themselves with the country of their adoption, they, too, became builders, and the style of Byzantium, rather than that of Rome, was the one which most commended itself to their taste. And so the traveller finds a third style of church in North Italy, that still called the Lombard. These churches are cruciform in plan, and domed, after the Byzantine style; they retain, however, the apse of the basilica, and the respective positions of altar and stalls; also the arm of the cross opposite the apse is lengthened into a nave; the apse itself, in a Lombard church, is always in the eastern position. The Lombard artist, too, was no timid sculptor, but on to these dignified outlines, derived from the two imperial seats, and in vivid contrast to them, he carved according to his proper taste the most fantastic of designs, rich foliation deeply cut, mixed with grotesque animals, birds, and human figures. San Zeno, in Verona, is rich in instances of this interesting outburst of sculptural invention; Lucca also; our church of San Frediano possesses a lintel over its main western entrance that is a fine example of the Lombard sculptor's workmanship.

San Frediano also provides us with another interest-

SAN FREDIANO. EXTERIOR.
From a photograph by Alinari.

ing architectural form, and one of purely Lombard origin. After the eighth century, bells were introduced into Italy from Greece for purposes of worship, and the problem was presented to the architect how to place them, and what architectural form was calculated to hold them to the best advantage. Square towers of defence were common in every city. Some few of very early date may still be seen in Florence; a splendid group still stands together in the centre of Bologna; while the little city of San Gemingano, among the hills above Siena, has a wealth of mediæval towers, singularly untouched. What form could be better than this to elevate and carry a church's bell? and turned from military to ecclesiastical purposes, what opportunity it gave to the eager Lombard artist to exercise his fancy and vigorous invention! At least, seeing the two orders of tower, side by side, one can hardly fail thus to speculate as to the genesis of the bell-tower. But whether this theory of its evolution be correct or not, the campanile became, and still is, one of the most striking features of Italian architecture, particularly where the Lombard influence was exerted, and may be seen in every degree of simplicity and richness. In that of San Frediano (see Illustration 2) we have the beginnings of a lighter and more decorative treatment. In the leaning tower of Pisa we see even impressive grandeur achieved, while under the hand of Giotto, and his successors, the Campanile in Florence became a thing of such exquisite beauty that perhaps nowhere, in all the world, is an architectural production which combines so many elements of loveliness, and presents a whole so nearly perfect.

The Campanile, then, is a usual adjunct to a Lombard church, and these two, with the Baptistery—another distinct building—complete the Lombard ideal of ecclesiastical requirements in architecture. The three, as grouped at Pisa, form an architectural whole unsurpassed in all Italy.

Again, later, when the north had developed its own Gothic, builders from across the Alps came with their northern ideals of architecture into Italy, and were from time to time welcomed; but never was the Gothic, as we know it, properly assimilated in Italy. The classic, the Byzantine, with the Lombard combination of the two, always held the Italian heart, and it is, for the most part, northern modifications of these that one meets with in Italy, rather than pure Gothic, free, vigorous, and untrammelled.

These then, broadly speaking, were the styles in architecture that engaged the minds of Italian builders at the time when the great period of Italian Art opened—the latter half of the thirteenth century—and they continued to hold their sway from this time on to the *cinque cento* (sixteenth century), when mediæval tradition was swept away in favour of the

[1] An example of the changed Renaissance style may be studied at home in our own St. Paul's.

BUILDERS AND GOLDSMITHS

new Learning of the Renaissance.[1] And it is owing to these diverse influences that we see so many, and such startling contrasts among the buildings of Italy north of Rome. But once let us perceive where these differences have their respective roots, and the apparent confusion becomes an orderly and rational development from natural causes.

On these buildings, thus conceived, the wealth of sculptural and pictorial art, which we northerners generally associate with the name of Italy, was expended.

And now, for the moment, we must turn from the consideration of these arts in the abstract, to the workers in them—the actual men whose hands and brains carried them on step by step, raising them from crude forms, and decaying tradition, to a new creation, the glory of their age and country, and excellent to a degree, that forces us to look back on them, with the same respectful admiration that their first builders looked back on the architecture of ancient Rome.

This great awakening, heralded as it had been by some centuries of architectural activity, took place first at Pisa.[1] Passing eastward over Lucca, Pistoia, and Siena, it reached Florence, and Florence, awakening with a will, stretched out her hands and embraced the rest, and became the metropolitan city of Italy in

---

[1] The pulpit in the Baptistery of Pisa is the first great work in which the new life is manifested. Its sculptor, Niccola Pisano, is called the father of Italian sculpture. A cast of this work may be seen in the Architectural Court of South Kensington Museum.

the matter of art. The highest artistic developments in Italy were all influenced, directly or indirectly, by her, and so all may, with hardly too much laxity of speech, be spoken of broadly as Tuscan Art.

And this suggests a further question. Why was this so? Why in Tuscany and its borders should this awakening have taken place, and spread from city to city, rather than in Calabria, Naples, Lombardy, or any other region which had once known classic influence, and that possessed relics of antique art to stimulate invention?

If we consult a map of the ancient world, we may find our answer. Modern Tuscany, with a wide border round it, corresponds to the Etruria of the earlier time. Comparatively little, up to the present date, is known of the ancient Etruscan in the days of his independent political existence, before the dominating Roman came and stamped him and his civilisation into the ground. But from the remains which still exist, it may be gathered that, like the Greeks, to whom the Etruscan people may have been racially allied, they were a nation of artists—sculptors, and vase-painters—and, above all, consummate workers in metals. In this latter art of the smith they surpassed in delicacy of execution and design even the Greek workman. A piece of Etruscan goldsmith's work, such as may be seen in various collections which have been lately made, is to this day a marvel

BUILDERS AND GOLDSMITHS 25

of delicate and artistic workmanship.[1] This people, though politically annihilated by the Romans, did not as a race die out, but remained on the soil, and, there is reason to suppose, singularly unmixed with the various other peoples which overran the peninsula. The mediæval Tuscan thus, with little admixture, was the descendant of the old Etruscan.

When the Tuscan artists began to work as Builders, as we have seen, they reverted, humbly enough, for the most part, to classic tradition and example. In Imperial Rome was the best that the world had seen of scientific building, and with the glamour of the Empire over it, the style appeared to them all-sufficient, and the best that could be; they were, in the realm of architecture, content to copy rather than to originate. But when they came to the more delicate work of decorative detail, there Rome had never been supreme. The antique sculptured capital they had worshipped once, finally failed to satisfy. Here, in these more delicate arts, their originality might have play with advantage; creative force, in fact, imbued them, and would out. Here they reverted rather to racial instinct—the old Etruscan in them came to life —with loving delicacy of hand and eye, supreme once, they would be so again. The fineness, the precision, the finish, their race loved, after the lapse of a millennium, lived again. The goldsmith in them awoke,

---

[1] The collections of Signor Castelani in Rome, in the new Gem Room in the British Museum, and that of Mr. Baxter, lately bought by the United States Government, may be named as among the best.

and the goldsmith touch was in their fingers, no matter what art they pursued. In actual fact, if we study our Vasari, we shall find that, among the earlier Tuscan masters, the art training of the greatest, with few exceptions, was literally in a goldsmith's shop—the shop of the working goldsmith who supplied the ecclesiastical, civic, and domestic demands of the time, for ornament in precious metals, jewels, and gems.

But "goldsmith" is a term which, in mediæval times, conveyed a wider meaning than it does to-day. Perhaps the profession generally has reached the low-water mark of all time, in this our proud Victorian age. The mediæval goldsmith was an architect in miniature; he was not a mere setter of jewels for rings and brooches, but a designer of complex forms for most multifarious uses; he employed his gold and silver, his gems, enamels, coral and the like, not so much to display wealth, as to display workmanship, as materials to carry out his design; the metals for his constructive lines, and lineal decoration, the rest to introduce colour and richness, where such was demanded by the nature of the work. He was a veritable artist in the strictest sense of the word, the same in kind as the architect, sculptor, or painter, less only in degree. A certain French archæologist, in this connection, writes :—

"Transport yourself to the epoch when Christian art could realise its plans with some fulness, and we see how in its speciality—the great cathedrals—the work of the architect and that of the goldsmith were combined, to ennoble men's minds by awakening in them the sentiment of infinity through the aspect of the beautiful. Note that there are two infinitudes in nature—as below the great infinitude is to be found the infinitude in miniature. And these two extremes should be reflected more than anywhere else in the art whose object it is to awaken in man the remembrance of God. . . . This in sublime emulation, art—bold copyist of the Creator—knew how to imitate in the religious edifices of the Middle Ages. Penetrated with the sentiment of divine immensity at the aspect of a cathedral, when you approached the Holy of Holies, did not a new world in some sort open before you? Above your head were suspended the broad crowns of light, near by, the great candelabrum spread out its branches, over the altar rose the ciborium, where the dove hovered; the cross crowned the dome . . . a tablet of gold, lustrous with precious stones, formed the front of the altar, and the reliquaries of the saints shone out in a circle from the depths of the sanctuary. Now, what was an antique reliquary but one cathedral enclosed within another? The equivalent in the world of miniature infinitudes, to that which the earth has of most perfect in the world of great infinitudes. Therefore as the more you contemplate the work of the architect, the more beauties you discover in it: so the more closely you study the work of the goldsmith, the more you will perceive new riches of beauty."

At home, in the South Kensington Museum, are many small examples of ecclesiastical goldsmith's work of the Middle Ages, Italian and other. In Florence, in the Museum of the Duomo, is a splendid instance, an altar front—once in the Baptistery—all of silver. The whole beauty is in the workmanship and the design, for neither enamels nor precious stones are used at all. Five or more artists laboured upon it, and begun in 1366, it was not completed until 1480. It presents a striking example of architecture in miniature. In the centre is a niche, holding a full-length figure of the Baptist; on either side of this, and at the two ends, are ranged panels representing scenes from his life. Each panel has a deep setting of architecturally designed mouldings, and the whole is held together by a rich, overhanging cornice. Magnified, it might, with modifications, almost serve for a gloriously rich cathedral façade. As for the detail, the sculpture within the panels is of no modest aim, nor feeble execution. The entire altar is a great achievement, the work of sculptors, draughtsmen, and designers of no mean order—in short, it is the work of mediæval goldsmiths of the Tuscan race.

Naturally, however, the material used was often of a less costly nature than gold or silver, yet whatever the material, this goldsmith's standard of workman-

BUILDERS AND GOLDSMITHS

ship was maintained, and the marble monument was practically goldsmith's work in stone. The training in the one art prepared a man for all. Brought up as a goldsmith, a youth naturally learned to draw, had practice in design; it was necessary further that he should model and study artistic construction; thus the most thorough and catholic training in the practice of art was given in a goldsmith's shop. After passing through that training, the Tuscan youth who had a spark of genius within him felt that he might safely apply himself to any branch of greater art.

The shrine or "arca" of San Dominico in Bologna is an interesting instance of what may be termed goldsmith's work in marble, so delicate is it in its design and execution. It, like the Florentine Baptistery altar front, is not the work of one man; it is, in fact, a co-operative work of art, which gives it a strong human, in addition to its artistic interest. Again five names are associated with it, and these worked on it at intervals over a period of about three hundred years. The sarcophagus itself, begun about 1267, is said to be the joint work of Niccola Pisano himself, and his gifted pupil Fra Guglielmo; certainly one can trace in it the masterly sense of proportion which was so characteristic of Niccola, and at the same time the sculptural delicacy which always marks the work of the monk Guglielmo. Between 1469 and 1473, a certain artist called Niccolò carried the design further, added various architectural features, and surmounted the whole with wreaths and cherubs, very skilfully combining his later with the earlier Pisan work. His four years' labour here seem to have been the great event of his life, for his name is handed down to us as Niccolò dell' Arca. He did not, however, complete his design; some figures were still lacking when he retired from the field. So, when in 1474, it was known that there was a young Florentine sculptor of promise in the city, having been obliged to leave his own home owing to political disturbances, the Bolognese invited him to contribute two of the figures to their great arca. He did so, an angel on the right-hand side and a figure of St. Petronius over the sarcophagus, and so the arca obtained the added distinction of having upon it work from the hand of Michel Angelo. The first and the last of the giant race of Tuscan sculptors here meet on the tomb of San Dominico—Niccola Pisano and Michel Angelo.

But in Florence itself, as one would naturally expect, is to be seen perhaps the most perfect specimen of goldsmith's work in stone. This is the tabernacle in the church of Or San Michele, and is the work of one of the greatest of Florentines, Andrea Orcagna (Illustration 3). The scheme of thought worked out in this great monument will be spoken of at length in another place;[1] it is touched upon at

---

[1] See "Further Notes for Travellers," a "Florentine Masterpiece," page 174.

Plate III. To face page 30.

ORCAGNA'S TABERNACLE IN OR SAN MICHELE.
From a photograph by Alinari.

BUILDERS AND GOLDSMITHS 31

this point solely with reference to its rich and delicate workmanship. It was a labour of ten years (1349–1359), and is a large monument rising up almost to the vaulting of the church. The whole is a fretted network of white marble, the interspaces filled with precious stones and enamels of all colours. The columns are spiral, and twining around them are jewels, while the top of each is surmounted by a figure of saint or angel carved in marble ; other figures in relief command the corners, in groups of five ; a further series of reliefs runs round the base, yet with all its richness there is about it a certain masterly restraint. The whole, with its carving, its jewels, its architectural lines and its colour, is veritable goldsmith's work, and yet is architectural to its topmost pinnacle.

Passing mention may also be made of another sculptural work in Florence of most finished delicacy —the pulpit in the church of Santa Croce, the *capo lavoro* of Benedetto da Majano.

Reference has as yet only been made to examples of sculptural art ; further on, in our examination of the subject we shall see the same delicacy of workmanship exhibited in painting, and it will then be even more clearly perceived how intimate was the relation of the Goldsmith to all the arts, and how he, with the Builder, laid the foundation for one and all. The Roman arch-builder of the Colisseum and the aqueduct on the one hand, and the Etruscan worker in precious metals on the other, by the process of time merged into one, and became the Tuscan artist. The Child of History and the Son of the Soil was artist innate, and out of his nature sprang that "new sweet style" in art as in poetry, which we now look back on with such wonder and admiration.

Still another point must be considered in our attempt to gain a clear idea of this period. It is, roughly speaking, one of three centuries, from 1250 to 1550; in these years all that was best in Italian art was produced. During this time the presence of three great and characteristic forces must be clearly perceived. First, that of Art, which flowed freely and spontaneously in the full current of the people's life, materially colouring it with its own rich tincture; and further, in the channel of general thought, were two other streams—the one Religion, expressing itself in the fashion of the mediæval church; the other, ever gaining strength with the advance of time, was the New Learning, itself a revival of the wisdom of antiquity, notably that in the works of Plato. Art, the Church, the Classics formed the threefold source of the intellectual life of the period, and it was for the first to take the last two for its material on which to work, and by so doing to give them outward and visible expression.

To grasp all that this means would be a lengthy task, and to enable the reader to do so would be altogether beyond the aim of the present work; but to ignore the presence of these elements altogether, in trying to understand the art of this period, would be as it were to plant ourselves with short-sighted eyes before a rich and varied landscape, and neglect the optician's aid to our defective vision.

A middle way may perhaps be found that will serve our purpose of laying a foundation to further study. To this end, let us choose a time fairly midway along the course of those three great centuries, and look if we may find a person embodying the characteristics above indicated—a man of strong artistic genius, delicate in workmanship, noble in temper, and expressing his nobility in the religious fashion proper to his time, and withal open to the beauty and the influence of the New Learning. Such a person, could he be found, might surely be considered as representative in broad lines of his time.

At a date sufficiently near the central point of our period, there does, in fact, occur in the annals of Italian art the name of a man who, for the most part, fulfils our above-stated requirements. Sandro Botticelli, the pupil of Fra Filippo Lippi, was the child of his age, *par excellence*, and in his work we see all the great forces of his time intermingled, determining its scope and range, and yet withal his own strong individuality gleams throughout, and gives a special and deeply personal character and charm to all that he did. He served the orthodox apprenticeship to the goldsmith, before he embraced painting

c

as his profession; he was profoundly impressed by the doctrine of the great Savonarola, and at the same time, his ears were not closed to the teaching of the New Learning, which in his time was in its brightest days, flourishing under the influence of the magnificent Medicis, and their new Platonic Academy.

Of Filippo Lippi, his master, Browning, in his "Men and Women," has given us a picture that apparently breathes with life. Taking Vasari's account for his basis, he has drawn his portrait of the artist brother, of a monk without a vocation, whose heart beat somewhat too wildly under his conventual frock for his own happiness, or for success in his enforced line of life, and who broke bounds and lived clandestinely the life of a careless libertine. The painter himself, however, has, perhaps unconsciously, left on record in one of his works some indication of his ideal of woman, and his notion of a man's attitude before his ideal; neither of these is that of a libertine. In the academy in Florence is a large painting by Lippi of the Coronation of the Virgin (Illustration 4). Christ and His Mother occupy the centre of the composition; around, in orderly and adoring groups, are angels and saints, while, mingling with the crowd of faces, in a sweet profusion, are white Madonna lilies; the whole seems seen through a maze of lilies. The man's full strong life flows through the work with a sense of joy in the celestial, and enjoyment of the earthly glory. Down at the bottom, however, is

Plate IV. To face page 34.

BUILDERS AND GOLDSMITHS 35

introduced a secondary interest, as far as the composition is concerned, but of great interest otherwise, since it obviously strikes a personal note. Beneath the angels and the saints kneels a girl, entirely human, devout, placid, sweet and very lovable; even in her prayers her sympathies are not closed to her surroundings, and little babies at her side do not fear to catch and hold her fingers, while she strokes the cheek of one of them with her disengaged hand. Behind the girl, just within the picture, well in the background, is a man in monkish dress; he kneels as is fitting before the vision of the Madonna; his eyes, however, are not fixed upon the crowned Queen of Heaven, but rest quietly upon the girl.

We are told that, as a culmination of his ill-doings, Fra Filippo fell in love with a novice, and daring the public opinion of the day, persuaded her to forsake her convent, and then married her. Tradition adds that this sweet, though inattentive worshipper of the Madonna, is a portrait of the ex-novice. Though a comparison of dates disproves this latter tradition, the picture none the less shows the type of woman whom the artist cared to paint with delicate care and exquisite sympathy, and also the attitude with regard to her which he thought suitable for the man, all of which points to a character in the painter different from the one so lightly attributed to him by Vasari; and when we hear that a Papal dispensation was finally obtained to legalise his union with the runaway novice, one cannot but feel that that, too, speaks strongly in his favour.

However all this may be, a man of strong virility and of warm human sympathies, as well as of orthodox training in ecclesiastical art, must have been Fra Filippo, the master under whom Botticelli placed himself in order to study the art of painting, after having passed through his apprenticeship in the goldsmith's shop. Thus, at the outset of his career, the imaginative genius of Botticelli was disciplined and braced, first, by the goldsmith's training, and then by the companionship and teaching, of the ex-monk. It soon, however, became apparent that his aims in art were on a higher plane than those of his master, and that even in technical matters he took Fra Filippo's lessons, and expanded them into a grace and wealth of craftsmanship the monk's hand could never achieve. A picture now in the Uffizi, in Florence, "La Fortezza," or "Fortitude," painted while he was still a youth, gave strong indications of what was to follow from his hand, and also shows the temper of the lad. This is a work which most English visitors to Florence take pains to see, sent by Mr. Ruskin's directions in his "Mornings in Florence." The subject, "Fortitude," is represented by a single female figure, sitting on a marble seat in an architectural niche. The general effect, at first sight, is probably startling, until we realise that it is the work of a boy, and then, irresistibly, we are constrained

BUILDERS AND GOLDSMITHS 37

to admire, if not the picture, at any rate the boy. He could not have been painting very long when he produced his "Fortitude." We see that the proportions of the figure are somewhat lost under the drapery; the hands, always a tremendous test, have been almost too much for his powers of draughtsmanship, though, despite faulty drawing, he has managed to project into them much character and meaning. Of figure drawing, evidently Fra Filippo had still somewhat to teach him, but of the knowledge he had gained before he placed himself under Fra Filippo we see much display, in command of hand and delicacy and precision of line. It would be hardly possible to treat drapery or architectural lines more severely, though in perspective these latter are faulty. The goldsmith's apprentice does credit to his training, and we see how he brings into his painting what Orcagna and the rest preserved in their architectural and sculptural designs. As to the intellectual insight which the lad brought to bear upon the matter he had taken in hand, it may perhaps be permitted to quote a paragraph from Mr. Ruskin:

"I promised some notes of Sandro's 'Fortitude,'" he writes: "I've lost my notes, and forget whether she has a sword or a mace—it does not matter. What is chiefly noticeable in her is that you would not, if you had to guess who she was, take her for Fortitude at all. Everybody else's Fortitudes announce themselves clearly and proudly. They have tower-like shields, and lion-like helmets, and stand firm astride on their legs, and are confidently ready for all comers. Yes; that is your common Fortitude. Very grand, though common. But not the highest by any means. Ready for all comers, and a match for them, thinks the universal Fortitude; no thanks to her for standing so steady then. . . . But Botticelli's 'Fortitude' is no match, it may be, for any that are coming. Worn somewhat, and not a little weary, instead of standing ready for all comers, she is sitting apparently in reverie, her fingers playing restlessly and idly, nay, I think even nervously, about the hilt of her sword. For her battle is not to begin to-day, nor did it begin yesterday; many a morning and eve have passed since it began, and now, is this to be the ending day of it? And if this, by what manner of end? This is what Sandro's 'Fortitude' is thinking. And the playing fingers about the sword-hilt would fain let it fall if it might be; and yet how swiftly and gladly will they close on it when the far-off trumpet blows, which she will hear through all her reverie."

All this was the lad's work, at any rate, able to suggest to Mr. Ruskin, and as one looks at the quaintly drawn, yet beautiful picture, one feels that our English interpreter may indeed have entered very nearly into the mind of Sandro as he painted his "Fortitude." He was no mere painter-craftsman, but a painter-poet. And yet, withal, he was, and in this also representative of his time, no college

THE MAGNIFICAT. BOTTICELLI.
From a photograph by Alinari.

BUILDERS AND GOLDSMITHS 39

graduate, nor gentleman in any technical sense whatsoever, but a genuine goldsmith's apprentice, not having even a surname of his own inherited from his father. Such a beginning gave glowing promise for the future, and Sandro in no wise belied this promise of his youth. In the Uffizi, hanging on the same wall as his "Fortitude," is a large circular picture, known as the "Magnificat," a work of his maturer years (Illustration 5). For this no apologies are needed on the score of unskilled shortcomings. One feels before it that, for its particular style of work, it is the best that can be done. Fra Filippo, churchman and lover though he was, never painted Our Lady as she is represented in this work of Botticelli. The pupil's intellectual conception of the subject far transcends the highest efforts of his master. Mary, here, is not a merely passive handmaid of the Lord, but a woman of lofty capacities, fully conscious of all that her great destiny means for her, and raised by it to a regal dignity which is yet as humble as it is majestic. The attendant angels of this group are of great interest. The peculiar type of celestial inhabitant, as seen in this work, is Botticelli's special creation, and these are perhaps his most successful examples of his chosen type. No other painter has conceived the angel in just this form—that of the beautiful youth, grave beyond his years, with an aspect of serious comprehension of the inner meaning of the scenes in which he takes part.

Other masters paid much less attention to their angels. Fra Filippo, for example, generally painted mere children, winged and rose-crowned; even Fra Angelico, who, if any one, should have delineated the perfect angel, paints an abstraction rather than a person. Botticelli's, though scarcely human, are distinct personalities. One can hardly reject the fancy that he owed his conception to Savonarola's dream of transforming the boys of Florence into God's white-robed messengers. The scenes which George Eliot so vividly describes in the pages of 'Romola' Botticelli lived among; his ears actually heard Savonarola's great voice in the Duomo, and, poet-painter that he was, he may have seized on the preacher's idea, and, as was not possible to the poor human and fallible little boys of Florence, he realised it in his art.

The delicacy of touch, the precision of line, which is noticeable in the "Fortitude" is also present here, and carried to a far higher pitch. True to his early training, Botticelli revelled in delicate manipulation, transparent veils, embroidered borders, just visible starry crowns, these in actual gold, which glitter to this day—in all these he had no rival, and in this particular work they are most marked features, while the sweeping lines of the whole composition, which hold it together, and give such complete satisfaction to the eye, are essentially sculpturesque; one does not wish to add to, or take from, a line.

Another point in this picture may be mentioned

BUILDERS AND GOLDSMITHS 41

for the special purpose of the moment, taking it as a representative work of a representative man, and that is its landscape background. Quaint it appears to English eyes, but largely because our eyes are English, and not Italian; for it is but a slightly idealised Tuscan scene, and might stand for any part of the Val d'Arno. In this Botticelli does according to the custom of his time. The setting of the scenes depicted in Tuscan art was homely enough to the Tuscans, and the more one becomes acquainted with the natural features of Tuscany and Central Italy, the more one appreciates how closely the Tuscan masters studied Nature as she presented herself to their eyes.

In common with all the noblest intellects of the Renaissance, the influence of the New Learning upon Botticelli was to add to his mental equipment a new world of thought and imagery, without wresting from him his older intellectual inheritance. He never painted pseudo-classic gods and goddesses, and on the strength of these thought himself a Greek, after the manner of later artists. He took thoughts and motives from classic literature, and then clothed them with forms all his own, and made them vehicles for conveying his own meaning by suggestion or allegory. His "Birth of Venus" and "Spring," in the Uffizi and Academy in Florence respectively, are among the most important of his paintings under classical influence. In the National Gallery we have a "Mars and Venus," a piece of exquisite draughtsmanship and quaint fancy. But we have the good fortune to possess also in the National Gallery, one of his most lovely works under Christian influence—a gem of double value, from the point of view of its artistic excellence, and as showing much of the inner working of the painter's mind; for, after all, he was always more profoundly Christian than neo-pagan.

The work in question is a "Nativity," painted with that peculiar delicacy of which he, among all goldsmith painters, was the chief master. The Holy Family is under a slight shed, the beasts bowing before them, and the shepherds and magi adoring. Streaks of golden glory mingle with the discoloured straw of the thatch, upon which are angels singing; and above, descended from the dome of heaven, in the light dancing motion Botticelli so loved, are other angels circling hand in hand, while at the foot, hiding from before the face of the Divine Child, are demons, crushing themselves out of sight, under rocks and stones. In front of these, introduced quite arbitrarily by the painter's fancy, is another group of beings, half of them celestial and half human—angels and men, who embrace and kiss—the former bearing leafy branches, which may be either the olive of peace, or the myrtle of love. Peace and good-will, the Highest come down among men, earth and heaven in one supreme moment blended and at one, is the sentiment of the picture. And if, in Milton's great ode, the

BUILDERS AND GOLDSMITHS 43

immortal story may be said to be told in organ tones, Botticelli has transferred the theme to the stringed instruments—soft, delicate, throbbing with intensity, and with human feeling. "This Lyric of Redemption," the work has been called, and that fittingly. Into some such train of thought and exalted mood, does Sandro's work lead any one who looks on it with sympathy. But the careful examination of Mr. Sidney Colvin has given us, in addition, a further insight into the meaning intended to be conveyed by the painter. Introduced into the painting is a Greek inscription, which, as deciphered by Mr. Colvin, reads as follows :—

"This picture I, Alessandro, painted at the end of the year 1500 in the troubles of Italy, in the half time after the time during the fulfilment of the eleventh of John in the second woe of the Apocalypse in the loosening of the devil for three and a half years. Afterwards he shall be chained and we shall see him trodden down as in this picture."

In the painting alone we see very clearly the temper of the man and the trend of his aspirations ; but here, by the light of his quaint inscription, we see further—even into his intimate thought, his outlook upon his age, and the meaning that it had for him. It is made obvious that in contemporary events Botticelli read the fulfilment of the Apocalyptic vision. The eleventh chapter of the Revelation tells of the preaching of the two Witnesses, and their deaths by reason of the war made against them by the Beast. The great events which had just passed over Florence were the "witnessing" and consequent deaths of Savonarola, and his faithful follower Fra Dominico by order of that most infamous of Popes, Alexander VI. To the devout and mystic artist, follower of Savonarola, who himself interpreted the Revelation in the light of current events, these things could not but appear as prophecies fulfilled; and if so, further fulfilment must reasonably be expected—Divine judgments on the wicked, and a final triumph of righteousness—and so, in faith and hope, he painted his "Nativity." Alas, poor painter! his dream may still be seen, one of the priceless treasures of Trafalgar Square, but the fulfilment is not yet.

Perhaps it was the depression consequent on hope deferred, even in his own time, which dimmed the lustre of his last years; be that as it may, he almost laid aside his art as he grew old, and in the end died lonely and poor.

CHAPTER II

DREAMLAND AND REALITY

WE have seen in the last chapter, first, the prime importance of Building to all great art, and to a certain extent the influences which determined the style of the buildings in Italy; and then, that for them, such as they are, in their excellences and their defects, were executed the further and greater works of art in Sculpture and Painting. We have noted the influence of Imperial tradition upon the artists, and also the deeper hold of their newly awakened racial instinct,—and now must be considered to what subjects the artists turned their attention, and the manner of their treatment of these subjects.

Once, in the National Gallery in London, the following was overheard. Two persons, having entered the gallery, placed themselves before the "Nativity" of Botticelli, mentioned above. "See!" exclaimed in tones of admiration the one who was evidently the guide for the occasion. "Yes," replied the other slowly, and then after a considerable pause, "But it couldn't possibly have been like that really, you know—I've been to the East, and I know." And so saying, the visitor doubtless expressed the opinion of many another, and further said what was literally true. Yet, in the opinion of all those best fitted to judge, Botticelli's imaginative presentation of the scene has that in it of value which no wealth of antiquarian and local accuracy could ever give; and so the question arises, wherein lies this value? The present chapter and the next will be devoted to answering in some measure this question.

Once having the attention turned to the matter, it will be seen that, broadly speaking, subjects for art may be treated in two ways—either from the standpoint of the realm of imagination, or from the standpoint of literal fact. Now as to the first of these— the standpoint of the realm of imagination,—we must all be conscious of a certain dreamland of our own, in which things and ideas are pictured in our minds, not necessarily as they really are, but as we should like them to be, and as they might be, were our mutual relations different; or again, the ideas which picture themselves so clearly in our minds may be of such things as cannot be in actual reality, under conditions of flesh and blood, time, gravitation and the like, and yet they are no less mentally real to us. The pantomime transformation scene is a crude and mechanical attempt to make concrete our childhood's dreamland of fairies and fancies of that nature. A matured and refined imagination creates nobler dreams, however, and instinctively desires

DREAMLAND AND REALITY

their realisation, the which may be effected in another fashion—in short, by the way of Art, which can give form and reality and expression to even dreams. Then, when we come to the act of thus realising dreams by the way of art, we find that what we need above all else is to gain the reality we seek, by an expression of the *spirit* of our idea. The figures must be arranged, the accessories added to emphasise and elucidate the idea—judiciously, irrespective of the actually and physically possible. Thought transcends the material. Hence gravitation, astronomy, chronology and the like are not to be too rigidly considered, the laws of any or all may be interpreted at will, or even skilfully violated, so long as the idea is made plain. To make an example of such treatment,—suppose it were desired to express in artistic form some one of the great ideas which are growing in the social conscience and imagination of the present time, let us say respecting Womanhood. We might introduce in a representation of such a subject as types, or as forerunners, or as in some way bearing on the idea, the Virgin Mary, Joan of Arc, Michel Angelo's "Aurora," Mary Wollstonecraft, and any modern and still living representative woman. All might be in one group, in sublime indifference as to the impossible chronology of such grouping, and to the fact that one of the number never was woman at all, but only a great man's idea of woman. What we wish is to express our dream, so with propriety we may take, and that together, the singer of the Magnificat, the inspired warrior, Michel Angelo's ideal, and a living object of our admiration, if any or all express some aspect of that dream. It may be light that has no relation to the sun which glows upon, or even from their faces, they may stand on earth, or sail in clouds, according as the one position or the other expresses the sentiment which we desire to have expressed, and as we have the art and the skill to express them. This done, with art, no one can say us nay; we have expressed our idea, and it was that which we set out to do. Ideas, real and true as ideas, but abstract in their quality, can have no photographic actuality in their presentation. The abstract cannot be photographed, and yet may be represented, and when done in masterly fashion, the highest form of art is produced, that which is called the Ideal.

Continuous delineation of the unseen, however, is beset with dangers. It not being possible in the nature of things to bring these works in their entirety up for judgment before actual fact, the artist may stray so far along the path of conventionalisation that he may end in symbolism rather than art, a condition fatal to all fresh invention and profound beauty; or he may become so wildly fantastic as to reduce his work to absurdity.

The second standpoint mentioned, that of Literal Fact, produces the Realist in art, and his is the

DREAMLAND AND REALITY

natural counteracting influence which holds the light up to the Idealist, to remind him that a measure of truth to the actual, must underlie all his dreams, or he will defeat his own ends. The Realists, too, "the artists of observation," as they have been aptly called, produce also an art of their own, strong and wholesome, commending itself to many, but of necessity somewhat more limited in its scope than that of the true Idealists.

Both these forces, Realism and Idealism, innate in humanity, were active among Italian artists, acting and reacting upon each other, and often together in the same individual. Thus, in considering Italian art as a whole, we must always bear in mind that there were the dwellers in dreamland, whose aim was to make visible their dreams, and who studied nature to that end; and there were the lovers of reality, who sought primarily to reproduce what they saw. In this connection, it is of immense interest to examine the drawings, sketches, and studies of the old Italian masters. The gallery of the Uffizi is very rich in these. We have also a collection in the British Museum, while the Royal collection at Windsor includes some of the brightest gems of the Masters' drawings that are in existence.

Passing now from the general to the particular, when the Italian Idealist of the Middle Ages came to make visible his dreams, of what nature would they necessarily be? Obviously, as ours are of the possibilities, the hopes, and conceptions of our times, so his were of the beliefs, the faiths, and ideals of his time, modified, as is the case with us, by the personal character and environment of the artist.

To bring this out with greater clearness, we will again take a specific example, in the person of one man, to represent an order of mind. Of all Italian Idealists perhaps the most complete was Fra Angelico (1387–1455), monk of the Dominican order, in Savonarola's convent of San Marco, in Florence.

Apart from his work as an artist, Fra Angelico's life was singularly uneventful. He entered the Dominican order at Fiesole, which from its hill overlooks greater Florence, nearly, let us say, as Highgate overlooks London. It is interesting to note in passing, that Fiesole was an ancient Etruscan town,—remains of this older period may be seen there to this day.

Trained as a miniaturist and an illuminator in the convent scriptorium, Fra Giovanni, to give him the name he chose himself on entering his order, soon showed capacities for work on a larger scale, and when removed to the then newly renovated convent of San Marco, he was employed to decorate its walls with frescoes.

An incident touched with a quaint mediævalism is told of this period of his career. The Pope heard of his skill as a painter and the pious spirit manifested in his work. The death occurring of the Archbishop of Florence, the Pope invited Fra Giovanni to fill the vacant office, reasoning, curiously enough, that so religious a painter must needs make a good bishop. Long did the humble brother pray to be excused this honour before the Pope would give up the idea. "He who practises the art of painting," pleaded he in his embarrassment, "has need of quiet, and should live without cares and anxieties. He who would do the work of Christ must dwell continually with Him." Happily, in the end he obtained his wish, and posterity has been enriched by the art which he was thus left at liberty to produce. According to the rule of his order, he travelled from convent to convent, and always in his journeys he prosecuted his art. His most notable works, out of Florence, are at Orvieto and Rome. In the latter city he died. He did not confine himself to fresco—that is, painting on the plaster of the wall—but also executed many easel pictures, these all more or less in the miniaturist style, delicate in line, brilliant in colour, with few shadows, and much gold introduced into the backgrounds. One such, of exquisite beauty, we have in the National Gallery. After his death he was "beatified," while it would seem that even during his lifetime his monastic name of John was almost lost in the affectionate title of "Angelico," bestowed on him by those who knew him. His full name, as finally recorded, carries with it quite a history of the man. It runs: "Il Beato Fra Giovanni Angelico da Fiesole"—the Blessed Brother John the Angelical, of Fiesole. With a sweetness of manner far beyond the ordinary, and of apparently a strongly monastic temperament, Fra Angelico seems to have almost realised in his own person that character indicated in the pages of the "De Imitatione Christi." But, withal, he was an artist, a great one, a dreamer of dreams. Then, what would naturally be the character of the dreams of such a man? The "Divine Comedy" of Dante gives us the outlook of the mediæval scholar upon the universe; and Fra Angelico, the monk, had devout belief in this divine order — that the theological system overshadowed and included all things else, and was of all things the most deeply real. Among these mystical realities the painter lived, and it was dreams of these to which he gave visible form. His words, "He who would do the work of Christ must dwell continually with Him," strike the keynote of his life, and he looked upon his works as direct inspirations from God, never altering nor improving his designs when once they were drawn out, saying that such was the will of God.

For nine years he lived in San Marco, the brother angelical, and breathed, as it were, in fresco on to its walls, otherwise so severely plain, his spiritual visions, so that to-day, the convent, suppressed as such, exists as a shrine of ideal art surely the most pure and heavenly that man's hand ever has produced.

Without frames or gildings or setting of any kind

whatsoever, these frescoes spring as by magic from the simple plastered walls. Two lunettes in the cloister are of special interest : they illustrate the virtues of Silence and Hospitality, both of which were particularly enjoined on the Order. The Silence is singularly simple in its lines and conception, and yet it forcibly arrests attention. It is merely the half-length figure of a Dominican, with finger on lips. To understand its full significance we must remember that Angelico's dreams were very real to him, and in his scheme of the universe the " Dominicani," "dogs of the Lord" as they loved punningly to call themselves, were an integral part, and necessary agents in bringing about the final consummation of all things. Silence, he represents then as no impersonal nymph in mountain solitude, but as one of themselves, on whom that discipline was specially laid. A Dominican he painted, but a hero of the Order, St. Peter Martyr, who had lost his life on a mission against heretics. It is he, the perfected brother, with the signs of his martyrdom just indicated, who looks down with a warning glance upon the cloister walk, and with finger on lip reminds any hasty brother, " Remember, silence ! "

Even to a nineteenth-century tourist, the fresco is impressive. The " Hospitality " is very tender and graceful ; two brothers of the Order, with faces of angelical guilelessness, and with eager outstretched hands, welcome a rough-clad stranger, with a sad, quiet face, and a pilgrim's hat slung across his shoulders. Apparently they see only his weariness and need; but Angelico has painted above the pilgrim's hat the cross-shaped nimbus, and thus applies his lesson.

In the Chapter-House is the chief glory, a large fresco which occupies the whole of one wall, representing the Crucifixion.

This is a striking instance of a dreamland presentation of the spirit of the scene, with no attempt to realise it as it had happened in actual fact 1400 years before. To Fra Angelico it was a fact of eternal significance; having happened once, it transfused all time, and was the keynote of the Universe. This sacrificial fact alone is that about which the painter here concerns himself; what to him is mere dramatic incident, or chronology, or such minutiæ? The great Idea dominates, and everything else is introduced to emphasise that idea. It is as Dr. Burckhardt writes, "A mournful lament of the whole church, here assembled at the foot of the cross, in the persons of its great teachers and the founders of Orders." Thus we have a group at the foot of the cross, with Mary as the principal, then to the left stands John the Baptist the Forerunner, then two Evangelists, and lastly three Martyrs; on the other hand St. Dominic kneels closest to the cross, and following him come Sts. Ambrose, Augustine, Jerome, Francis, Benedict, and others, ending up with again

DREAMLAND AND REALITY

members of his beloved Order, the Saints Peter Martyr and Thomas Aquinas.

Passing upstairs to the dormitories, at the entrance one is confronted by an "Annunciation," fitting commencement to a series, one in every cell, of scenes from the Life of Christ. The older painters, and least of all Fra Angelico, were not antiquaries in their method of picturing scriptural scenes: they had not been to the East, and never dreamed of making their pictures oriental; but the sacred stories were to them very sacred, very real, and of eternal value. The Virgin, then, Fra Angelico conceives in this Annunciation, sitting in a cloister, as it might be the one below in his own convent, and the angel, such as he believes to be all around, only to us invisible, comes, and in her cloister, visits her. This angel is a characteristic example of his conception of celestial inhabitants, and very unlike Botticelli's angelic youths. Fra Angelico's creation is of beings neither male nor female, with strange rapt expressions, caught, as it were, from a perpetual sense of the Beatific Vision. There is an exquisite grace in this angel of the Annunciation, his reverent, and yet half-wondering salutation to the simple maiden, who perfectly represents the spirit of her reply, "Behold the handmaid of the Lord." So begins the series, and with the same touching grace and charm it is continued. The coronation of the Virgin, and the Transfiguration being perhaps the most lovely, the two subjects the most removed from earth and things real, they defy description, and, alas, also reproduction. The photograph is absolutely inadequate to convey an idea of these particular frescoes. The stiffness of the drawing is faithfully rendered, but shadows are unduly exaggerated, and the absence of colour, so great a feature in Angelico's work, make a reproduction absolutely misleading. His easel pictures, with their richness of gold and colouring, may be transported to foreign galleries: these may even be photographed with a certain measure of success, and their loveliness thus may be enjoyed away from their birthplace. But the frescoes of San Marco, labours of love for his brother Dominicans, and having a special charm above that of any of his more public works, can only be seen in their home.

In the Last Judgment, however, a comparatively small work preserved in the Academy in Florence, we see the master in one of his highest flights. It represents the scene, of course, conventionally; or rather, it is a presentation, within the limits of pictorial art, of the spiritual signification of the Judgment. Readers of Dante will feel that here is the Divine Comedy in miniature, the literal presented for the sake of the great allegorical meaning behind, and yet though literal it is not, as indeed it cannot be, realistic.

In the centre is the Judge, immobile, placid, not hurling denunciations in his own proper person, but

PARADISE. FRA ANGELICO.
From a photograph by Alinari.

DREAMLAND AND REALITY

merely giving expression to the eternal Law of Consequence. Around him are "the bright seraphim in burning row," while behind is indicated the ineffable light, which screens the Beatific Vision. On either side are the Fathers and Doctors of the Church—Mary and John Baptist head these two rows, while seated at the ends, on either hand, are Sts. Dominic and Francis, the founders of the two great preaching Orders. The last Trumpet has sounded—the celestial trumpeter is yet in position below the throne—the graves, a row of flat-topped tombs, stand still lower in the centre—and judgment having been pronounced, the Blessed and the Cursed go to their respective fates. A crowd, more or less confused, is on the left hand, mingled with fantastic, goblin-like demons, who hound the lost souls on—here one sees a monk rending his frock, which has proved no cloak to his sin; there a miser with now valueless money-bag; tonsures, crowns, mitres, cardinals' hats, great folk and simple—the single-eyed Angelico groups all together; but having so placed them, on the dolorous left hand, he can do no more, his pencil and invention alike fail. The Inferno is the unspeakable to him. He hastily indicates the final goal—hardly more than as in a diagram—and that done, turns with relief to the other side, the dreamland of his heart's desire. And nowhere in all Italian art is just such a presentation of celestial joy (Illustration 6). In most works representing Heaven and Hell, the latter is made the more interesting of the two — action, expression, dramatic incident, contrast, variety, are all more or less admirably given. The pain and horror have stirred the artists' imagination, and commanded their highest efforts. It is so in the Pisan sculptures, which adorn the great front of the Duomo of Orvieto, —also in Luca Signorelli's frescoes in the same church, to which reference will be made later; while the bliss of the accepted ones, though probably as devoutly believed in, they were not inspired to depict. Their efforts resulted in a certain fixed monotony, or strained ecstasy, too placid or too forced to interest. Fra Angelico, however, turned to the Paradise as to his spirit's home, and to him it was given to conceive forms of joy, purely celestial. His Heaven is all strictly within artistic limits, but infinite in its suggestions of joy and welcome, reunion, compensation, and increasing Beatitude, and all drawn with a quaint grace, wholly unearthly, and yet not unhuman.

But to enjoy the full significance of the works of Fra Angelico, and notably this "Giudizio Finale," one must for the time being throw aside all private opinions, conclusions, and attitudes, and for the nonce become, as far as in one lies, a mediæval Christian. Our neo-mediævalist poet, Christina Rossetti, must surely have had his works in her mind, as she wrote the following verses, which breathe the spirit of Angelico, and specially that infused into the work of his which we possess in the National Gallery :—

> "Multitudes, multitudes, stood up in bliss,
> Made equal to the angels glorious, fair,
> With harps, palms, wedding garments, kiss of peace,
> And crowned and haloed hair.
>
> Each face looked one way, like a moon new-lit,
> Each face looked one way toward its sun of love;
> Drank love, and bathed in love, and mirrored it,
> And knew no end thereof.
>
> Glory touched glory, on each blessed head,
> Hands locked dear hands, never to sunder more;
> These were the new begotten of the dead
> Which the great birthday bore."

In the year 1447, Fra Angelico was invited by the Cathedral authorities of Orvieto, to undertake the decoration of a new chapel in the south transept. According to the complete fashion of the day in Italy, walls and ceiling were to be alike frescoed, one whole scheme of thought to run throughout. Giotto's little chapels in Santa Croce in Florence, are excellent examples of this finished style of painted decoration. The "Spanish Chapel" in Santa Maria Novella, in Florence, is another instance on a larger scale. So complete and rich is the painting that it is all-sufficing, and sculptural accessories are not needed in the scheme. The walls, left simple in construction and line, give the painter all the fuller opportunity; and when, as in these instances, he has had a free course to the end, the result more than justifies the plan—it is of an exquisite richness which completely satisfies.

The Cappella Nuova at Orvieto was to be another great instance. The subject was the Judgment—the end of the world—the walls to have represented on them the final scenes of the great world drama—the overthrow of Antichrist, the sounding the Last Trump, and the dispersion of the risen souls into the two bands of Blessed and Cursed; while the ceiling, in its turn, was to have for subjects the Christ as Judge, and the Blessed in groups of Apostles, Prophets, and Saints in glory. "Generally in good Italian decoration," writes Mr. Ruskin, "the roof represents the constant or essential facts,—the walls, consecutive histories arising out of them, or leading up to them." The decoration of the Cappella Nuova in Orvieto is planned out on these lines. The dramatic scenes preceding the end, are represented on the walls, the eternal glory on the roof.

For three months, Fra Angelico worked here, and painted the Christ, as the central figure of the ceiling, opposite the entrance, and two of the groups of the Blessed; three panels altogether, in the vaulting. These completed, and apparently some further cartoons drawn out, he was compelled to leave Orvieto, and it was fifty years before the officials of the cathedral again lighted on a painter quite to their mind, to complete the decoration of the new chapel.

DREAMLAND AND REALITY

In the meantime the world had moved on, and it is curious to note on whom, when the time came, their choice fell, to carry on the work after Il Beato Fra Angelico.

In this interval of fifty years, Florence, Mother of the Arts, had passed through the remarkable period when Lorenzo de' Medicis, and the intellectual group he gathered around him, exerted their great influence in matters of Learning and Manners and Art; after that time, none of the three, and least of all Art, could ever again be entirely the same.

The cry under the teaching of this New Learning and of the works of Plato, in particular, became "Let us see things *as they are!*" "What *is*, is that which it is important to know:" and artists in consequence studied their art from a different standpoint. They could no longer be merely exponents of mediæval thoughts and spiritual dreams — improving their methods only so that they might make their meaning a little clearer and more forcible; or even if their subject were ostensibly of this older school of thought, their method of attack became different. The *manner* of the doing became in itself as important as the *subject*.

This New Learning, so called, was after all but a re-discovery of the old, the learning of the classic world of ancient Greece and Rome. Among scholars, it had the effect of turning them one and all into enthusiastic antiquaries. Antiquarianism with them, however, was in no sense a mere elegant pursuit, which may or may not supplement the labours of the historian—it was, in the early days of this new birth, literally a seeking for Dante's "pane degli angeli"—angel's food—the intellectual bread of life. The old scholastic learning had had its day and almost more, and at the time now come, could not supply the intellectual needs of humanity. It had been of value in its own day, one is apt at the present time to ignore of how great value, and what powerful intellects had been engaged in its pursuit. Yet, notwithstanding its worth in certain aspects, it had had a share in snapping the thread of tradition of scientific thought and investigation begun among the ancients, substituting for this a system of thought built up on premises, in their turn founded on authority alone. But when authority becomes dubious, what of the systems built upon that authority?

The pages of Plato showed comparatively firm ground upon which to stand, and a method for further and future progress. It is difficult to realise to-day the wild enthusiasm with which this New Learning was hailed as life and liberty to body and brain; manuscripts were searched for as for hidden treasure, and brought from ancient seclusion in Greece and Byzantium, and when possessed, were learned off by heart, copied, translated, edited, printed, discussed, and set up as standards of taste and style, and even of life itself. And these antiquarian researches were not confined to manuscripts alone—anything from the antique world was viewed with loving and with reverent eyes, and works of ancient art were seized upon by art students and lovers, as, what indeed they were, treasures inestimable. Lorenzo the Magnificent, among princes, was not unique in his possession of a collection of antiques—the artists themselves, as they could afford, became collectors. One of these— Squarcione of Padua, risked a voyage to Greece itself, in order to gather at first hand specimens of Hellenic workmanship, and on his return, threw open his collection as an art school. To this act of Squarcione was owing the education of the great Andrea Mantegna, less only than the four or five greatest artist giants of the period. In Florence was Lorenzo Ghiberti, the maker of the great gates on the east side of the Baptistery, which Michel Angelo named gates of Paradise—he too had his collection. An ardent lover of antiquity, he gathered together Greek vases, Roman bronzes, a number of marble statues, and other works of art. His enthusiasm was great and discriminating. Describing the statue of a Hermaphrodite, which had been recently discovered, he burst out as follows: " To express the perfection of learning, mastery, and art displayed in it is beyond the power of language—its more exquisite beauties could not be discovered by the light, but only by the touch of the hand passed over it." Again, on the discovery of another antique statue at Padua, he writes: "This statue, when the Christian faith triumphed, was hidden in that place by some gentle soul, who seeing it so perfect, fashioned with art so wonderful, and with such power of genius, and being moved with reverent pity, caused a sepulchre of bricks to be built, and there within, buried the statue, and covered it with a broad slab of stone, that it might not in any way be injured. It has very many sweet beauties, which the eye alone can comprehend not, either by strong or tempered light, only the hand by touching finds them out."

Ghiberti (b. 1378, d. 1458) and his contemporary Donatello, were of all Florentine sculptors the most fine and subtle in their execution, and as one reads his pages, one can almost see the former, passing his appreciative fingers over the delicate antique workmanship, humbly recognising all its excellences, and, for the nonce, in its presence, forgetting that, of which otherwise he was fully conscious — the exquisite delicacy of his own work.

Squarcione and Ghiberti were not singular in their attitude of admiration for antique art. The vision of it affected all workers in art, in a greater or less degree. While the preaching of Savonarola made some of the painters "Piagnoni" like Botticelli, Lorenzo di Credi, and Fra Bartolommeo, and reminded every one that there was after all in the old faith that which was worthy of their highest efforts, yet they could not see these "very many sweet

DREAMLAND AND REALITY

beauties" of the old world, without trying to bring some of them into their own work.

But the question arises, where specially were these "sweet beauties" manifested in ancient art? A few hours spent in the Greek rooms of the British Museum will supply an answer, clear and distinct—it was in the Human Form—"pure form nakedly displayed, and all things exquisitely made." The newly studied Plato declared that it is only a barbarian and debased taste which demands clothes—that the pure form given us by the gods is our most worthy covering; and in the ideal games held in his Republic, the ideal form, kept beautiful by Greek gymnastic, was to be unclothed; and so they found in all the highest Greek art the worthiness and beauty of the human form realised. The face may be conventionalised, and generally is—often into a sweet nothing—but on the body the Greek artist expended his powers of vision and dexterity. There was his art. This the Renaissance artists began to realise, and they ranged themselves one and all, in the *method* of their art, on the side of the so-called "Humanists."

One of the first who began to work along these new lines was Luca Signorelli; and as Fra Angelico may be considered the idealist *par excellence*, so may Luca be placed among the realists. Signorelli was born in 1441, and thus just overlapped Fra Angelico's last years. He showed little pietistic charm in his early works, but from the first he had a certain breadth and strength in his manner of working. When then the Time Spirit seized him, his was the spirit to mate with it, and express its teachings in art, and thus he found his place in the ranks of his craft. When he had reached the age of fifty-eight, and his style was well matured, while his hand was yet firm, upon him the choice of the authorities at Orvieto fell to complete the decoration of their Cappella Nuova, begun and left unfinished fifty years before by the Beato Fra Angelico.

Thus curiously, and with an element of strong interest to those who concern themselves with the development of Italian art, are brought into close proximity in one small chapel, the works of the two painters, at the extreme poles of that art.

Il Beato, as stated above, had, before leaving the work, completed three groups in the vaulting, and left designs for the remaining compartments, while the scheme for the whole had apparently been fully determined upon. The completed compartments, in their style entirely characteristic of the master, were painted in clear tints on a golden background. In this choice of gold—in the first instance a survival of the goldsmith in art—he may possibly have been confirmed by the glory of a sunset sky. At any rate, on seeing it, that glory is suggested to the observer; but the celestial glory being thus interpreted by gold leaf, no realistic effects of atmosphere were aimed at. It is merely a blaze of gold, nor is there anywhere the attempt to be at all naturalistic. In the assembled groups of the Blessed, no longer inhabitants of earth, no effects of earth are employed in the representation. In shadowless [1] glory they are grouped with a certain gentle austerity, one might almost say rigidity—and this is intentional, for Fra Angelico could portray emotion and action when he wished, as is clearly demonstrated in the figure of San Dominico in the Crucifixion in San Marco. But here in these groups of the Blessed is an intentional stillness, partly necessitated by their architectural position, and partly to convey the idea of the super-terrestrial. The painting is entirely angelical.

After this beginning, Signorelli followed on. For the rest of the vaulting he apparently used Angelico's designs, already alluded to, and loyally tried to preserve the older spirit in his execution of them. But the humanist painter is obviously ill at ease in these spiritual regions; and it is when the vaulting is finished, and he comes to the walls, that one sees him in his own proper atmosphere, and in full contrast to his predecessor in the chapel.

Apparently, the first of the series is on the right hand of the entrance. "The trumpet shall sound, the dead shall arise," he has taken, so to speak, for his text. Luca here is endeavouring to see things

---

[1] This absence of shadows in Fra Angelico's paintings of heavenly groups is noteworthy, and in accord with Dante's reiterated statement as to the absence of shadows among the inhabitants of the spirit world.

as they are, and he does so uncompromisingly. Poised in mid-air, stalwart angels blow a blast such as might indeed conceivably waken the dead, and these—some are mere skeletons, some with full covering of flesh—arise from out of the earth. His subject is a grand opportunity for realising the truth of the human form. To realise what the figure is, in proportions and parts, is the first step to making it beautiful, and here one sees with what earnest labour this early humanist studied with that intent. In this fresco is left aside all spiritual significations—that was old-world lore to Signorelli—he designed groups of absolutely nude figures, their thews, sinews, action, and the foreshortening of drawing are general and paramount. This is no dreamland representation of the judgment of souls—it is, in very deed, and in a double sense, the resurrection of the body. It is wonderful workmanship; one sees in it the technical parentage of much of Michel Angelo's work. There is character, force, and truth-seeking in every figure, and sometimes grace. Suppose an actual and material resurrection of the body, it might as likely be in this fashion, as conceived by Signorelli, as any other. Here is reality! A prophetic photograph, so to speak, of what might be, but nothing of dreamland, nothing of suggestion; Signorelli will have things *as they are!*

In the next fresco (Illustration 7) we see the Cursed on their way to the Inferno, as usual, hounded down by devils. In the upper portion of this picture

Plate VII. *To face page 68.*

THE LAST JUDGMENT.   LUCA SIGNORELLI.

DREAMLAND AND REALITY 69

are placed some military angels to overlook the execution of the judgment pronounced, while the mass of the composition in the lower half is a tumult of hunted souls, a barbarian battlefield rather, defeated and conquerors mingled with every sign of fear, horror, rage, and cruelty. The demons are not fantastic goblins, but hideously human. There is no faltering here in detailing horrors; Luca depicts them with an apparently inexhaustible invention, but they are physical horrors, as of the battlefield—it is pain, and struggle, and impotent rage, before invincible strength. That is the sentiment of the work. The qualities at which the painter aimed are totally different from those in Fra Angelico's Last Judgment. All through the writhing mass at the bottom of the composition is the carefully studied human form. Disentangled from the rest, each part is some portion of a figure accurately studied, carefully thought out—no difficulties are cloaked by mere drapery, it is indeed " pure form nakedly displayed." A step farther, however, must be taken before in art again is reached the " all things exquisitely made." No one, however, can fail to appreciate the interest and excitement here, though it is of so painful a kind. Signorelli's Hell is sufficiently horrible to satisfy the most exacting demands. One can imagine the Shade of Angelico overlooking him as he brought out point after point of horror, whispering to itself, " How *can* he do it all ? How can he bring himself to picture it with such terrible reality ? "

After the Inferno follows the Paradise (Illustration 8), and here the painter has introduced other elements, with fine result. The wild craving for thews and sinews is somewhat chastened, his groups are drawn together into a more ordered composition, certain of the angelic figures are lovely in their grace and the flowing lines of their drapery. One feels, in looking at this, in the presence of a great work of decorative art—splendid in line, in colour, and masterly in execution. But as a conception of Paradise! —no, its very realism robs it of reality. His angels are after all but majestic women, withal somewhat weighty for their seats of cloud, or for their wings to bear. The souls below are in ecstasy truly, but except for the indication in the name "Paradise" one would be uncertain as to whether of joy or pain. The contemporary artists, however, must have looked on the work with enthusiastic and unqualified admiration. "Surely here, and here," they would think, as they glanced at one figure after another, drawn with such mastery, "here we are at last realising the Greek standard, the human form is living again in art!" though the Shade of Angelico might ask, as it turned frozen with horror from the hell, "But can this indeed be Paradise? No, surely. *I* know what goes to make God's heaven, and it is not here!"

It is by another standard we must judge Signorelli and his like in art. He looked for outward truth

Plate VIII.

To face page 70.

PARADISE. LUCA SIGNORELLI.

DREAMLAND AND REALITY

and achieved it, and all honour to him; without him and others of like mind, there could not have been the final triumphs that we see in the works of the succeeding generations. As to the pleasure to be derived from these works, it must always be a matter determined by temperament. All, however, must concede that in his own field Signorelli was great. But obviously his was not a culminating point in Italian art. He was as a signpost, rather than a goal. Truth must be sought; what had been done in ancient times must be striven for again; figures must not continue to be swathed in drapery because, forsooth, the painters could not draw them; they must be real, real as truth and earnest study could make them; but yet by them the Ideal must also be expressed, or else art would indeed be stricken in part dumb. And so, as we search in the galleries at home and abroad, we see that after Luca Signorelli, artists did not stand still. He was not the last of the Realists, any more than was Fra Angelico the last of the Idealists. Knowledge and imagination came together, and of their union sprang greater works than either of these painters could have believed possible, or perhaps could have understood if they had seen them.

CHAPTER III

DREAMLAND AND REALITY (*continued*)

IN Luca Signorelli and Fra Angelico we see two very pronounced types of mind—the one Realist, the other Idealist—each producing high forms of art, but at different poles of thought and aim. Any more ideal art than that of Fra Angelico can hardly be conceived, nor a more realistic treatment of the subjects executed by Signorelli at Orvieto, and yet they do not mark the limits of art. Both types are necessary for a wide and full national art; but for the topmost flights of that art, the two must be combined in one artist, and seen both together in his work, in all their respective excellences.

To illustrate this further advance, it will again be well to select one man, and examine certain aspects of some of his works; thus we may hope to arrive at a point whence, if so minded, we may proceed farther, and take a wider field for our observation. In this instance we will choose as our example of the Idealist and Realist in one, Raphael Sanzio; and for our present purpose we will, for the sake of clearness, confine ourselves to one element only in his

DREAMLAND AND REALITY

work, that of the Sky combined with the Supernatural, and trace to some extent his development of that element through a number of his works, from his student days up to his all too early death.

A background is an obvious necessity to all painting; and if we look at any representative collection of Italian paintings, ranging from early to late years, we may see that the question of background is one of gradual development, in idea as well as in execution. Very early Italian works have for the most part the goldsmith's background of gold, and very long was it in the annals of Italian art before the gold background was left entirely behind. As we have seen, far on into the fifteenth century, it was used by Fra Angelico, frequently and with wonderful effect, in expressing his celestial glory; even Signorelli so far yielded to the conventional as to use it in the upper part of his " Paradise," at Orvieto.

Among the first, if not indeed the first, to break through this rule was Giotto, and he has, in many of his most important frescoes, a deep, unbroken blue that cannot but have been suggested by that tone which the Italian sky takes in the height of summer, at the hour preceding sunset. And so, from Giotto onwards, gradually working its way into the minds of the painters, the sky and the earth asserted themselves as the fittest of backgrounds for human events. According to their respective temperaments, the different artists paid more or less attention to this element in their paintings, but in the end a certain excellence was attained; not that they rivalled the modern landscape painter, who studies Nature's every mood, catching at each passing effect of light and atmosphere, but the Italian generally arrived at a pleasant, true-seeming approximation, which, if it does not excite profound admiration, neither does it arouse carping criticism. It is easy to comprehend, the artist did not attempt more than he felt quite competent to do; indeed, in later days, he must have repressed himself in many cases, lest a too rich background should take away from the prime importance of the figures. And as with the landscape proper, so with the sky; it was more and more faithfully studied and represented, until it became a veritable sky, the beauty of which the artist fully appreciated. But with this growth of the real in the treatment of sky, a fresh difficulty arose. The art of the time was religious,—heavenly appearances and significations were demanded of it; with the carefully studied reality, it was necessary also to express dreams, and the completely abstract. At first this difficulty was hardly recognised as such; the two were simply introduced together arbitrarily, with no real harmony between them attempted; the reality of the one element in the work thus making the other stand out with the more startling unreality.

Pietro Perugino (1446–1524) gives us perhaps as good examples of this transitional stage as any

THE RESURRECTION. PERUGINO.

other. This painter of Perugia, in Umbria, arrived at an exquisite style of landscape and sky background. The enchanting loveliness of Umbrian scenery could hardly fail to make its impression upon any one who was at all sensitive to the various aspects of Nature. Perugino seems to have studied his Umbria to some purpose, and the broad characteristics of its scenery he almost invariably introduces into his backgrounds. Once having grasped the elements of his style in this particular, one can tell "a Perugino" almost at a glance. He became distinctly a mannerist, but in such a graceful style one can in no wise regret it. His skies are generally clear, gradually shading down into a sort of subdued glow towards the horizon, while a landscape is lightly indicated running into the picture in good perspective, some few trees being nearly always silhouetted against the sky. All these elements may be seen in a certain painting of his preserved in the Vatican Gallery, representing the Resurrection (Illustration 9). An early morning sky forms the background; in the foreground are the figures, in a beautiful group, drawn in masterly style. Christ rises from the tomb into the air; in front are two soldiers, still sleeping; behind are two others, one in the act of flight, having caught sight of the wonder. The figures are as studied as Signorelli's, but much more beautiful, nor is there any shirking of difficulties. Perugino has learned Florentine draughtsmanship, and has a grace peculiarly his own. But in spite of all the beauty of truthful representation, of masterly drawing and tender colour, there is a something in the work of quaint and archaic, which almost provokes a smile, and all the more because of the presence of so many excellences. Perugino came of a devout school of painting; devout and mystical dreams were among the elements of his art; hence much more must he put into his work representing the Resurrection than a mere group of soldiers, and a figure poised above the tomb. The heavenly and the mystical, in the midst of all this realised earth, must be made apparent; and he does this, so it appears, without perceiving the difficulty of the task, and with a quaint directness which is truly wonderful. We see uncompromisingly placed in mid sky, against the glow of dawn, attendant angels; under their feet are little strips of cloud, which but make their graceful appearance there the more unexplained. With Fra Angelico and other earlier masters, for example, the formal accessories are in harmony with the formal angel—there is a certain æsthetic proportion between the two; in such surroundings such visitants excite no surprise. But this work of Perugino is full of faithful study of nature; his angels are carefully studied, and so, though in themselves singularly beautiful, they are somehow incongruous, and the little clouds under-

DREAMLAND AND REALITY

neath their feet, like slender brackets against the sky, only serve to emphasise the incongruity, and their weight upon atmosphere. But stranger still, the painter has drawn around the figure of Christ, in a plain ribbon-like band, an almond-shaped glory, flat on to the sky. At once we are placed completely outside the realms of the real, and the work becomes, despite all its excellences, one that does not carry conviction; it is too real, or too conventional. The symbolical "mandorla"[1] is as out of place as the cloud strips are inadequate. Perugino has not solved the difficulty. The divine must be made to appear divine, he felt; to him and to his public the sacred symbol was as the A B C is to us; what better method, then, could be used in order to express his meaning than to place it frankly in his morning sky? Yet, by so arbitrarily and unskilfully introducing his dreamland into his reality, he, from the point of view of Art, spoiled both.

Perugino was the master of Raphael, and from the level reached by his master, the scholar-assistant made his start. By a stroke of luck, or by happy arrangement, in the Vatican Gallery there is hung

[1] The "mandorla," or almond-shaped glory, is in Christian symbolism and art reserved for Christ, and has a profound signification. Though called a mandorla, or almond, it is really intended to represent the form of a fish, and this, from the days of the Church of the Catacombs, was the accepted symbol of Christ, because the letters of the Greek *ichthus* = fish, give the initials for the Greek words, Jesus Christ, Son of God, the Saviour.

close to Perugino's Resurrection, an Assumption of the Virgin by Raphael (Illustration 10), painted in the period when working under the influence of Perugino. In this we can see the younger still following in the steps of the elder, yet with a certain individuality of his own. We have the same landscape background, running into the picture, with the silhouetted trees, but when the sky is approached there comes a difference. Evidently the student has felt the difficulty that the master has either not perceived, or by which he has been baffled. The picture is, as the subject demands, in two groups, the one, of the disciples on the earth, around the Virgin's empty tomb, and the other above, of the risen Madonna and the Divine Son, who receives her into heaven. One can almost trace the lad's thought as he worked out his picture in this matter of sky. If heavenly visions appear in clouds, he has thought, at least let us have a sufficiency of them, to give an appearance of reality to the whole. So, straight across the picture, greatly to its loss from the point of view of composition, he has placed a great mass of cloud, and to plainly show its solidity and thickness, he has even indicated its section! But Raphael is a dreamer too, he has his conception of the heavenly inhabitant, and of the beatified baby form he became the complete master. In this work one sees his early efforts. Some one or two of the attendant cherubs are already graceful in form, but others are

Plate X. To face page 78.

THE ASSUMPTION OF THE VIRGIN. RAPHAEL.

DREAMLAND AND REALITY 79

still very archaic. The blue sky rises behind the shelf of cloud, and studding this somewhat flat blue sky is an array of clearly-defined baby heads, which suggest the angelic host quaintly enough, how inadequately Raphael was perhaps the first to perceive.

Fortunately for him, a time soon came when he was able to leave Perugia and was free to travel—accordingly, we find him next in Florence, in 1504, twelve years only after the death of Lorenzo de Medicis. Here he became acquainted with the great art works in which at that time Florence was so superlatively rich, works of Leonardo da Vinci, of Michel Angelo, of Donatello and the rest, and thus he entered into the full current of the intellectual life of that day. Fra Bartolommeo became his friend, and under these influences, the genius of the young man went forward by leaps and bounds; for, away from the traditions of Perugino and the Umbrians, his own proper style began to emerge from those traditions. After four years of Florentine life, he was invited to Rome by Pope Julius II., the patron and friend of Michel Angelo. On arriving in Rome he was employed to decorate four large rooms or *stanze* in the Vatican for the Pope, and, in the first of these, it was designed to have frescoes representing theology, poetry, philosophy, and jurisprudence. He began with "Theology;" the "Dispute of the Sacrament" is the name generally given to this work, and it is painted in what is known as his Florentine manner, as distinguished from the earlier Peruginesque, and the later style, which he matured in Rome. Another name for the fresco, given with perhaps more discrimination, is "The Glorification of the Christian Faith." In the centre is the altar, and on it is displayed the Host, while grouped on either side are the fathers and doctors of the church who have expounded the Christian mysteries. Behind these comes a Peruginesque landscape, silhouetted trees and glowing sky, and then in a wide semicircle are the clouds which support an upper and celestial group of members of the Church Triumphant. Between the treatment of these clouds and those of the Assumption is a whole world of difference. The heavenly company in this case does not so much rest on them, as that the clouds form an edge to a region which lies behind. These persons have not come down out of heaven to rest on a scaffolding of clouds, but rather, behind the clouds, the heavens have opened and the eternally present—to Raphael—is for the moment made visible. Then as to the clouds themselves, are they indeed clouds? one asks as one continues to gaze, or is what we see rather a mist of angelic movement taking the form of clouds? For here, his cherubs no longer studding a flat sky, merge into and animate the cloud, and are thus at once more real and more ideal. So, under the sovereign touch of the young Raphael, the real and the ideal approach, without any seeming

DREAMLAND AND REALITY 81

clash. Here, too, we have the "pure form" in which if the subject demanded that it should be "nakedly displayed," we should find as in a Greek statue "all things exquisitely made." But with all the reality of the workmanship, the ideal predominates. Raphael has used all his knowledge of the forms of things that he may express their essence.

There is another point in this painting worth noting, though it has no reference to the matter immediately in hand, but since it indicates something of the personal character of the painter, it may not be considered foreign to our subject as a whole.

In the group of doctors of the church on the right are two figures not usually represented in such company. They are Raphael's own innovations. First and easily to be distinguished is Dante, introduced here as theologian rather than poet. But in the extreme corner is a black cowled head appearing behind the rest, and not so easy to recognise. Tradition, no doubt justly, says that this represents Savonarola. Only ten years before, Savonarola had been unfrocked, degraded, and hanged, and burned, in the open piazza in Florence, by papal order. More than half the people yet alive in Florence and in Rome when this fresco was painted, had heard at first hand, or seen with their own eyes that day's doings; for the four preceding years Raphael had gone in and out among them; Fra Bartolommeo, his chosen friend, was a *piagnone*, and Raphael the

F

dreamer and historian as well as painter could not have heard the tale without some responsive fire being kindled within him. This we see realised—for coming to Rome, to paint in the Vatican, Raphael places among the chief teachers of Christianity the so lately degraded and burned Dominican.

From the "Disputa" we will pass to a work separated from it by some years, the "Madonna da Foligno" (Illustration 11). Here the Madonna occupies the upper portion of the painting, while on the ground are saints and a worshipper. The whole, however, is not a "two-decker" composition, for the Madonna, though above the rest, is yet drawn well into the group, by the lower part of her drapery and the surrounding glory. In this case she is quite outside heaven, the sky has not rolled back, but she rests on an immeasurable depth of cloud; the ideas of bracket and scaffolding are quite left behind, the whole depth of the atmosphere is at her disposal, within which she rests and has the appearance of repose. The heavenly element is again suggested by cherubs, so slightly indicated as to be hardly distinguishable from the clouds. Again the thunderbolt introduced below is a realistic touch, in natural harmony with such profound masses of cloud. There is altogether a closer adherence to nature,—but a commensurate increase of art in the manner of that adherence.

Yet one farther step did the master take in this

THE MADONNA DA FOLIGNO.   RAPHAEL.

particular, as we may see in his last work of all, the well-known "Transfiguration." On this painting he was engaged at the time of his death; and when the young painter lay dead, the work, half finished, was hung over his bed; and with the colours still wet upon it, it was carried before his hearse, to his burial. The upper part is what he executed with his own hand; the lower was completed after his death, by his pupils. It is however with the upper part that we are concerned at present. In this the Christ rises in a mass of luminous cloud, and as it seems, by His excess of glory draws up with Him also Moses and Elias. This does not, however, take up the whole width of the picture,—a normal sunset glory shows to the right,—the world is going on as usual elsewhere—only to the few is the transfiguration made visible. The dividing line between the celestial glory and that of the sunset is masked with consummate skill by a tree, half lost on the one side in the brightness of the cloud, showing out on the other in almost the old Peruginesque style. In this last work the cherub even is discarded in suggesting the spiritual,—it, no more than the older "mandorla," is felt to be necessary. Here we have a restraint that is almost Greek. To express the most mysterious of scenes, the means employed are the simplest, only the cloud, and the Christ, and the glory of the two transfusing the rest, and yet by the art of Raphael the idea intended is expressed. The humanistic *vraisemblance* and the mystic unearthliness which had been separate and apart in the works of Luca Signorelli and Fra Angelico, here find a point of union, through perfect mastery of method and technique, guided by a lofty and noble imagination.

From a certain point of the Vatican Gallery may be seen, by merely turning the head, on one wall the "Resurrection" of Perugino above mentioned, with its harsh nimbus, and risen figure placed arbitrarily in the sky, its elegant angels, and little cloud strips, its quaint beauties, and still quainter incongruities—from the point of view of the present subject—and then on another side hangs Raphael's glorified Christ. The contrast, especially bearing in mind the historical link which binds them, is striking, and one of peculiar interest.

In the above slight tracing of the development of one aspect of art, in the works specially of one man, nothing more has been attempted than to be suggestive, and to indicate by the means of one example, that which runs through the whole of this outburst of art in Italy;—that this whole was built up by accumulated individual efforts, influenced by individual character, that it was a matter of gradual development through the interchange from mind to mind, of knowledge and idea,—in short, that Italian art, like every other great art, was in its time alive, a part of nature, growing out of the hearts and brains of living men.

DREAMLAND AND REALITY

Before passing on from this subject of the real and the ideal, we must touch upon yet another of its aspects.

The traveller in Italy is indeed unfortunate if unable to pass through Venice, while in every gallery of note some of the greatest treasures are specimens of Venetian art. When, however, we come to examine the art of Venice, we find ourselves in another world from the one developed under the influence of Florence. Venice was in its history much apart from the rest of Italy, and in art was singularly alone and untouched by the great Tuscan inspirations. Realism and idealism we see, as indeed we must in every art that becomes great, but in Venice the result is very different from that in Florence. Starting from a different standpoint, they aimed at a different goal. The Tuscan, using the word in its widest application, was always in his highest flights more or less of a mystic, the unseen and the abstract were always present to his mind; ideas enthralled him, and in his art he sought to realise his ideas, and at the long last, as in Raphael and Michel Angelo, realism but served to make the expression of the ideal more beautiful and more perfect.

The Venetian had his period of faith and piety, but the Unseen had not the same lasting fascination for him that it had for the Tuscan, and as the years passed over him, his endeavour became rather to bring all things down to the present and the actual, and for this he had some potent reasons. For what in the three centuries of which we are speaking was the present and the actual to the Venetian citizen? It was an ever-increasing material glory. Venice, unlike Florence and the other northern Italian cities, was not torn by factions, Guelph and Ghibilline, Blacks and Whites. It had not had its towers destroyed by one party, to be built up by another. With all its passionate life, it had held itself together, by itself and for itself. In its history few single names stand out from the rest of its citizens, so that, as it were, the city was but a setting for the citizen. Venice had no Lorenzo the Magnificent, no Savonarola; what Venice had was Venice, and her Sons were proudly content to be Makers of Venice, and with a glorious result. The "Bride of the Adriatic" is a city unique in the annals of the world. Lovely it is in its decay; no wonder that in the days of its glory it filled the imagination of its inhabitants, so that what they actually saw within it satisfied the desire of their eyes. And so their art, taken as a whole, tended to become but an added glorification of Venice, and of persons as inhabitants of Venice, and on the ever-present, and lovely vision of their own city, their idealism played. For idealism does not confine itself to one form of manifestation. We may, it is true, express the purely imagined, and give that form, but it is also possible, and, in fact, it is the more common form of idealism, to take the real and the actual, for the matter of our thought, and place it under ideal conditions. The family may be taken for example, or friends, and imagined as just lacking those defects which affection suggests are accidental rather than innate. In some such fashion, taking a larger field, William Morris conceived that charming dream, his "News from Nowhere." Its inhabitants are flesh and blood, and good English folk to boot, but yet, somehow, for the present at least, they exist in reality—nowhere. They are purely ideal, —in their way, as much so as Fra Angelico's angels.

So in like manner, in art, to a large extent, the Venetians looked on Venice and idealised it. A glorified Venice, an idealised life as lived in Venice, is their constantly recurring theme, and even when not the ostensible theme, one feels that that idea is in the background of the painters' minds, colouring their representation of any other subject which they have undertaken to execute. Thus it may be seen that, *while the Tuscans in their art realised Ideas, the Venetians idealised Reality.*

When one speaks of Venetian painting, at once there springs up the thought of the sumptuous, the opulent, the gorgeous, the idea of a full rich human life. As a natural outcome of their mental attitude, the Venetians excelled in portraiture, and their canvases glow with colour and light, and are magnificent in architecture of the richest, and draperies the most superb.

In the Academy in Venice is a picture representing "St. Clara" by one of the Vivarini, a group of the earlier masters of the school (Illustration 12). It seems, as far as one single work may be said to do so, to strike the keynote of the spirit of the art of Venice. In an early Tuscan work of a similar subject, there would probably have been presented the personification of some presumably appropriate spiritual attribute, while the robe and knotted cord of the Order would be made to serve as indications that the figure represented the first woman follower of St. Francis. This picture of Vivarini, however, is no personification, but, on the contrary, we see strong personality. One who in her youth had loved the young enthusiastic Francis, and for his sake left the world, and then wisely ruled and bravely defended her convent, and in mature years continued the friend and counsellor of her old lover, might just so have looked, as in Vivarini's painting. An elderly woman, he draws her, with strongly-marked features, speaking of great force of character and balanced judgment, intensely human, strong, and good. From just such a one could we imagine wise counsel being sent down to the cell by the Porziuncula, to clear up the maze of ecstasy and enthusiasm, which may well at times have clouded the brain of the poor, self-tortured Saint. This is a human conception, which has grown up in the mind of the master,—a portrait of his idea,—the

ST. CLARA. VIVARINI.

Plate XIII. To face page 80.

THE MADONNA OF THE TWO TREES. BELLINI.

St. Clara as he idealised her to himself, made visible.

Of their earlier religious art, Giovanni Bellini gives us the finest examples, and his acquaintance may be made at home, through some three or four works of great beauty in our National Gallery. He comes, in spirit, possibly the nearest of all to the earlier Tuscan masters, but at the same time exhibits a very marked divergence from them in method. This may be seen very distinctly in a painting in the Venetian Academy known as the "Madonna of the Two Trees" (Illustration 13). The Madonna is represented half-length only, and is seated in a beautiful and stately pose, with the child standing upon her knees; behind her is a simple, straightly hung curtain, and on either side a green tree. If one mentally compares this group with, let us say, the "Magnificat" of Botticelli (Illustration 5), one sees at once the fundamental difference there is between the methods of the two schools. In short, Bellini had not had the training of the Tuscan goldsmith; there is not in his work that delicate perception and free use of *line* which distinguishes the work of nearly every Tuscan artist. The Venetian is content with the majestic pose of his Madonna, the divinity of the Child, and the rich colouring of the robe, the folds of which are few and simple; they and the curtain alike are, beyond their colour, not further enriched. The Tuscan revelling in flowing, yet guided and disciplined *line*, is quite absent. Between the "Magnificat" and the "Madonna of the Two Trees" is a whole world of difference. In the former we see an example of what was the prime element of the art of Florence; before all things else, with the Tuscans, came *Form*. The arts of sculpture and painting walked together, one helping the other towards a mastery over, and perfecting of Form. As has already been noted, many of the artists were both sculptors and painters, and the severity and truth of drawing, necessary to all great sculpture, had its influence on their painting. If Giotto the painter gave a new impetus to Sculpture, the sculptors Donatello and Ghiberti, in their turn, infused new life into Painting. In Venice, on the contrary, there does not seem to have been this intimate connection between the two arts. The sculptural element can indeed hardly be traced in Venetian painting, which grew up not so much on the basis of Form as on the basis of Colour. Colour is the paramount element with the Venetian. From Colour, and from Light, their creations spring; Form follows after, to make the two former articulate.

The central figure among the creators of this art of Colour was Tiziano, or Titian (b. 1477, d. 1576), who must rank also among the greatest painters of the world. A pupil of Bellini, when he became a man, he quite put away the pious spirit of his master. The severe and the religious were not in accord with Tiziano's view of life, for he breathed to the full the glorious materialism of his city, in that day.

In the "Presentation of the Virgin to the Temple" (Illustration 14), now in the Venetian Academy, we find a work full of a personal interest; Titian seems to have reflected in it, as in a mirror, what must have been his thought, his temper, and his attitude towards life and things, while it also reveals what a consummate master he was in his art. A consideration in some detail of the elements of this painting will make this clear. The work ostensibly represents an incident in the life of the Virgin Mary. The story of the life and death of the Madonna is one constantly recurring as a subject in Christian art. Found in one of the apocryphal gospels, it is illustrated by painters and sculptors countless times.

Joachim and Anna, runs the story, were a childless couple in old Judea. They were pious, charitable, and religious according to all the law of Moses, and thus they lived together for twenty years, earnestly praying the while for the blessing of a child, and vowing that should their prayers be granted, the child should be dedicated to the temple service. But as years passed on, their hopes grew less, and one year, when approaching the altar in the Temple at Jerusalem, with his accustomed offering, Joachim was repulsed by the High-Priest, who refused the offering, saying that he must have sinned some great sin secretly, to remain thus childless in Israel. Joachim in grief and shame retired, not to his home, but into the wilderness among his sheep, and there mourned many days over his unknown sin. Anna, too, meanwhile wept bitterly, for since he did not return, she thought her husband lost.

But one day an angel of God appeared to both of them; first to Joachim in the wilderness, and bade him be comforted, for his wife, though now old, should by the power of God bear a child, who should be called Mary, and be specially honoured of the Most High, in that, in her turn, she should be the mother of the Messiah. Further, the angel commanded him to return home to his wife, who was about to set out to seek him, and meet her at the golden gate of the Temple. The angel then left Joachim to appear to Anna, and give her the same message and command. The husband and wife thus met at the Golden Gate, and had no need of speech, the love between them being so perfect that each knew what was in the heart of the other. In due time Anna became the mother of the promised child, who, according to the command, was called Mary; and when she was three years old they brought her with great joy to dedicate her to the Lord. There were fifteen steps around the Temple, according to the fifteen psalms of degrees, and, says the gospel, "the Virgin being

Plate XII.

PRESENTATION OF THE VIRGIN TO THE TEMPLE. TITIAN.

From a photograph by Naja.

placed upon the lowest step, ascended them all by herself without assistance, as if she had been of perfect age. And, after making their offerings, her parents left her with the other virgins in the Temple, and returned home. And Mary lived day by day in all holiness in the Temple in prayer and meditation, and study of the Word of God, holding converse with angels, and fed with celestial food from heaven, and increasing in stature and wisdom and grace before God and man."

Titian's painting represents that point in the story where the little Mary is making her unaided ascent of the fifteen steps. But, though that is the nominal subject, one cannot but feel that it is lacking in dramatic reality. It is obvious, in looking at this great canvas, that the story of the little Virgin, painted such innumerable times, from Giotto downwards, had ceased to interest Tiziano, and that what did interest him was the world around;—so here we have introduced into his "Presentation" all the elements of distinction in opulent contemporary human life. We have rich and scholarly architecture in familiar use; the people introduced, as if conscious of their worth, compose and comport themselves with dignity and propriety; their dress is just rich enough, and yet not too rich, and each figure has the strength and beauty of a self-respecting temperance. One beggar —not too miserable, however—is introduced to keep the whole within the bounds of truth to human society.

Then to fill up the measure of the general well-being, the glory of the earth is indicated in the landscape at the back—such a one as the painter knew well—a glimpse of the dolomites of Pieve de Cadore, his birthplace, and the home of his boyhood. The peaks rise up blue in the distance, with their whiteness just indicated here and there, while whiter villages shine out on the lower wooded hills. But it is, after all, a sacred story the painter has engaged to represent; so into his group of Venetian citizens gathered before the Renaissance Temple, one figure is introduced with the conventional drapery of the Biblical character, though he is not sufficiently individualised to name; and so the note is struck to show that it is intended to represent something more than an idealised picture of Venetian life; something—but perhaps not much more. For Venice, in its heart, at this time cared for none of these things, and we must look behind, to quite an obscure seeming person, before we find any one to whom the spirit of the scene is apparent. St. Anna, also in the background, watches her heaven-sent little daughter, and St. Joachim looks with understanding; a little girl at the foot of the steps has a quiet outsider's interest in one who was perhaps an old playmate, and two men behind the steps appear attentive; the old priest above is condescendingly benignant. The little Madonna herself is, however, wholly delightful—a perfect child; with a wholesome child's unconsciousness she goes up the

THE MADONNA OF THE HOUSE OF PISARO. TITIAN.
From a photograph by Naya.

steps, totally unaware of the halo round about her. So, as it were, in a quiet undercurrent, the spiritual is brought out, and that probably in a proportion to the rest of life, true to Titian's character and time. He knew of it, but was not possessed by it. It was the glory of the rich new life around him by which he was possessed, and perhaps little wonder, when we call to mind to what a pitch of loveliness those old Venetians had raised the surroundings of their daily life. So in exercising his powers of idealism, it was the daily seen reality which Titian idealised.

In the church of the Frari in Venice is another great painting, in which this same lordly citizen note is struck, and that even in the title of the work (Illustration 15). It is not the "Madonna of the Columns," or "Our Lady of the White Veil," nor any such name taken from a distinctive feature in the composition, as is generally the case with a Tuscan work, or even as we have seen with Bellini—no, this is the "Madonna of the House of Pesaro," and to the left of the picture, principal in the scene, are the representatives of the House. And these are not humbly waiting to be presented by some great saint, to the notice of the Queen of Heaven, but the great Venetian comes himself as of right to the great Mother; he comes worthily, he thinks, with his banner of victory and power, and his captive drawn after him. And indeed, looking at Tiziano's work, no reason is apparent why he should not so come. For as here depicted, though dignified and gracious, the Madonna is not the Queen of Heaven. The regal majesty, which the Tuscan conceived so nobly, is here quite lacking. Tiziano represents her as an idealised Venetian matron, that being apparently to him sufficiently noble for any sphere whatsoever. Another note, curiously interesting, is struck on the left-hand side, indicative surely of some attitude of mind in this man, who perhaps, of all others, painted for Venice. On this side, coming quietly, in startling contrast to the citizen pomp of the Pesari, is St. Francis of Assisi,—the coarse friar's frock, the stigmata, memorable signs of his self-discipline, are all there truly depicted, and with the glow of passionate asceticism on his face, and indicated by his gesture, he comes—he too—to the presence of the Divine Child. He comes and looks, and finds a mundane baby playing with his mother's veil, and holding out, for a familiar caress, its little foot, which Francis would hardly dare to kiss with a devotion never so deep. What did the painter mean? Was he covertly laughing at the whole matter which he was commissioned to paint? It is somewhat difficult to understand this splendid colour-dream masquerading under pious forms; but be it what it may otherwise, as a painting it is one of the most glorious of his most glorious age. As a work of art we cannot but feel that it is superb, everything about it is beautiful;—it flashes out from the wall on which it is hung, a

THE FEAST IN THE HOUSE OF LEVI. VERONESE.

From a photograph by Naya.

perfect masterpiece of painting. In the matter of composition it is noticeable that in this is a complete departure from the old balanced style of a central feature and two dependent sides,—as for example, a Madonna and two saints, the central Cross, and those of the two thieves. Here the figures are grouped diagonally across and up the canvas, which gives a wonderful effect of freshness and action to the whole. In short, the later Venetian painters seem to have struck out and away from all tradition, and, almost uninfluenced by sculpture, formed a grand style all their own.

But of all the great Venetians, the one who developed perhaps the most gorgeous style was Paolo Veronese. He revels in architecture, sumptuous feasting, magnificent textures, forms of noble men, and beautiful women. He is represented in our National Gallery, but naturally, he is to be seen at his best in Venice itself. The "Feast in the House of Levi" in the Academy, Venice, shows the principal characteristics of the painter (Illustration 16). One cannot for a moment imagine that the Gospel story was in his mind as he worked; he was no didactic painter of religious subjects. He merely takes this incident, or possibly the title only, to start from, and makes it the opportunity for a gorgeous composition, full, palpitating with the rich life he saw around him, this life taken at its best, and just so touched with idealism, as to make it even more gorgeous than the actual magnificent Venice. In Veronese, perhaps, more than even in Tiziano, one recognises the paramount position given to Colour in this school. To reiterate what was indicated above, while the rest of Italy made *line* their chief element, and strove above all things to draw, and to bring their compositions together, and produce a co-ordination of parts by means of a harmony of the lines, and then to this added colour,—the Venetians seem to have first conceived their work in colour and in light, and then added line. So, in the great "Feast in the House of Levi"—great in area as well as in quality—the whole is held together, not so much by the forms of the persons being in harmony with each other, as by a rhythmical arrangement of colour, which carries the eye along, and shows a bond which embraces the work and makes, of its separate parts, one whole. For instance, the Central Figure at the long table which runs across the picture, has a pale lemon-tinted halo; this colour repeated along the rows of guests to right and left, in tunic and mantle and what not, gives what is lacking in line, a sense of continuity of æsthetic thought, and a oneness, which satisfies even when one does not recognise what element it is which produces the satisfaction.

Having thus for the moment paused in thought before the art of Venice, with the endeavour through one or two examples to obtain more or less a key to the whole, we must like Dante, but for a reason totally the reverse of his, "having looked, pass on."[1]

[1] It must be understood that in thus taking our examples here and there, of artist or work of art, the intention is only to elucidate the matter immediately in hand, and is in no way an attempt to give a complete review of any one school or development of art. So to pass on from Venice without mention of Tintoretto is not to ignore one who was perhaps the greatest of them all;—only, to bring out the particular idea stated in the outset, the other painters appeared to afford illustrations more directly to the point.

CHAPTER IV

THE ARTISTS AS STORY-TELLERS

WE have now to take up another point. One of the functions of mediæval art incidental to the time, was the telling of stories. This in no way interfered with the primary functions relating to the Real and the Ideal,—it ran concurrently with them, and in fact gave these latter their opportunity. So all through our three hundred years, story-telling was one of the great works expected of artists, whether painters or sculptors.

This was incidental to the time, in that this time, for the most part, preceded that of printed books,— and entirely preceded the time of cheap and popular books.

It must not be supposed, however, that because of the rareness of books, this was of necessity a period of extraordinary mental degradation. The contrary would probably be nearer the truth; in any case, we may assume with much probability of being correct, that nowhere in Italy at the time under consideration, could be found such stupidity and mental

ARTISTS AS STORY-TELLERS

dulness as we may see to-day in our more neglected agricultural and slum districts.

The presence of books does not of necessity mean intelligence; there is no magical power in a book *per se* to diffuse sweetness and light. Literature, it must be remembered, is primarily but a method for the expression of ideas. In the middle ages, European literature was in its infancy; there was hardly the material then to compose the popular library, even if the necessary mechanical means had been invented. Thus in the nature of things the stored book-shelf was a rarity, the possession of either the scholar or the prince. But at the same time, the non-reading public was not necessarily a non-intelligent public; the people none the less thought, had ideas, desired these to be perpetuated, and to share them with their fellows. The portable cubic block of compressed thought—the printed book—was not, but there existed walls, doors, coffer-lids, panels, surfaces generally, and the passion for adding beauty to the same. Here then were the opportunities convenient for conveying thought, by combining that thought with the decoration then deemed necessary. The Italians were not as yet printers, but being artists, they blazoned upon those spaces their ideas; indeed hardly any object of daily use was considered fit to leave the maker's hands until it had some touch of art, added to its mere necessary form, to give it a further significance. Their whole outer life thus became tinged with their inward thoughts; these were everywhere, not shut up between book covers, but on every side, meeting the eye, coming under the hand; the unlearned could read this, the writing of the artists, merely by the exercise of the natural faculty of sight. Truly there were certain advantages in this older method of conveying ideas. If not compressed so as to be portable, they were diffused so as to be seen, and when seen we may be fairly certain that in general they were understood. The "public" of the mediæval artist was not the select few, but the veritable Public, the masses themselves; and it was from the masses that as a rule the artist himself sprang.

This being so, it becomes obvious, on thinking over the matter at all, what the subjects were that the artists received the commission to paint. For the sake of their intrinsic interest, and for the sake of the instruction that could be conveyed through them, they were those which at that day were considered of vital importance to society, and which in consequence had been made popular, viz., Stories from the Bible, the Apocrypha, and the Lives of the Saints; and later, when the New Learning advanced, to these were added stories from classic mythology; but these latter were secondary in the matter of number and popularity; the religious story, in accordance with the mind of the time, was always the most in demand, the story with its inner significance insisted upon by a wealth of symbol and emblem, well understood by the masses. The use of the "mandorla," mentioned above, in Perugino's "Resurrection" is a case in point, which, far from being unique, is rather typical of the artists' manner up to the period of the highest Renaissance development. For example, every saint had his and her accepted emblem,—Saints Francis and Catherine of Siena, the stigmata, St. Dominic, a star, St. Peter Martyr, the sword; the palm in the hand of any human person signified martyrdom, while in the hand of an angel, that he was sent as a messenger of death. A whole system of thought, with its own proper language, was common knowledge in that time, which we have in these days for the most part forgotten.[1]

Naturally, it was oftenest the walls of churches which were chosen for the artists to enrich with this more elaborate style of decoration. One example of painted decoration we have had occasion already to consider, that in the Cappella Nuova in Orvieto. This was a scheme of theological thought elaborately worked out; but in like manner, and more generally, some story was chosen with which to cover a wall, or even a whole interior. This was done most often in a long series of composi-

---

[1] A very helpful list of Christian symbols is given in vol. i. of Lord Lindsay's "Christian Art," and also in Mrs. Jameson's "Sacred and Legendary Art."

tions, carrying the story on scene by scene, many or few, from the beginning to the close, according to the taste of the painter, or the space at his disposal. Or, sometimes, if circumstances demanded, chronology would be more or less ignored, and a series of events would be arranged in one composition. This was a difficult task, at times, in the early days, producing a quaint enough effect; but later, when accumulated art gave greater power, under the hands of a master, a veritable masterpiece was the result, brought into such harmony that no shock whatever is given to the critical faculties, and insulted chronology smiles, unaware of the injury that has been done to it.

A prime instance of this form of continuous composition, or compressed story, is to be seen in the top panel, on the left hand, of Ghiberti's gates, for the eastern side of the Florentine Baptistery (Illustration 17). In the front of the composition, in the highest relief, is the form of Adam, to which the Creator is in the act of imparting life; behind, lies Adam again, asleep, while from his side rises the woman; still further into the composition is the Tree of Knowledge of good and evil, with the man and the woman beneath it; again, still further, is the gate of Paradise, and the angel driving away the disobedient pair; while, last of all, in the lowest relief, so as to be little more than drawing, is a mist of angels surrounding God the Father, who

Plate XVII.   To face page 101.

ARTISTS AS STORY-TELLERS

looks down from heaven upon the earth drama. Wonderful is the amount of incident compressed into this one panel; it is compressed, however, not crowded, and a more graceful composition could hardly be conceived,—it is, in fact, a triumph of art, with its various degrees of relief giving exquisite gradations of light and shade, and the whole held together with sweeping, yet disciplined lines. Every detail, even, is brought into harmony with the whole by means of its connection, or sympathy, with some one or other of the leading lines.

This form of sculpture, into which perspective is so freely introduced, is by some considered meretricious, and contrary to the canons of Art, and in the hands of other and lesser men it does indeed seem to be so, and such work is generally more or less of a failure. Ghiberti, however, by his complete mastery of technique, and his poet's touch, has overridden the canons, and, in spite of all, has produced what, in its way, can only be called perfection. He who of all men was best able to judge, and who, jealous for art, was not slow to criticise—Michel Angelo himself—gave to these gates the lasting name of "Gates of Paradise."

But to proceed. Sometimes it happened that the artist chose, or was commissioned to execute, a story of only local interest, and without special investigation, it is impossible to follow its details with full understanding, but this is comparatively rare. The above-mentioned sources supplied as it were the "stock" subjects which were of perennial interest, and continually in demand. The Bible in particular was always very fully illustrated, and as far as its principal stories were concerned, it was in no wise a sealed book, but an endless source of study. Perhaps of all the non-biblical stories, that of the life and death of the Virgin was the most popular, and after hers, those of the Saints Benedict and Francis, founders of monastic and preaching orders. So well were these and similar stories known, that they could on occasions be used slightly, as it were indicated as symbols of an idea, introduced in a secondary position, merely to emphasise the sentiment of the more important part of the decorative scheme. To take our example of this from a work already mentioned—Raphael's so-called "Dispute of the Sacrament" or the "Glorification of the Christian Faith." In this work the artist has achieved much, and suggested more, in his endeavour to express what he felt with regard to the Solution of Things as offered by the Church; and yet with all that he had done, he could not but be aware that even his masterly labour was inadequate; the subject demanded more than his powers could execute. How then indicate that after all, the Solution of Things is beyond complete expression? Running along the wall under the fresco is a band of ornament carried out in subdued tones, almost in monochrome, and into the ornament is introduced a medallion, and in that, lightly drawn, is the story of St. Augustine and the Child. The saint, so runs the tale, after labouring on his great theological work, went out upon the sea-shore to rest, yet still his mind was engaged upon the problem of how to expound the mystery of the Trinity. As he walked he came upon a little child who had dug a hole in the wet sand, and into it was pouring sea water from some little vessel. "What art thou doing?" asked the saint. "Trying to empty the sea into my little hole," answered the child. "Impossible!" cried the saint. "Dost thou not see? thy little hole contain the great ocean!" "Dost *thou* not see," asked the child, "how finite man cannot understand, much less expound, the infinite?" Augustine bent his head humbly before the reproof, and when he looked again, the Child was gone; so he returned home in the assurance that to him had been vouchsafed a heavenly vision. This then Raphael selected to supplement his great effort in the "Disputa," just quietly hinting thereby, in the ornament below, as who should say: "*I* know, despite all the praise given to me, I know, I have not said the half; the mystery is over and above the highest I can reach, with all my best endeavour."

Thus the Italian artist, whether painter or sculptor, when working at his best, interwove thought with thought, story with story, so that apart from elements and excellences purely artistic, requiring special gifts and training to appreciate, there was a world of interest in his productions, for every one who, in looking at them, would but at the same time think. It is not then enough simply to look on this picture or monument, and on that, and think that in so doing we have done it justice. It will be found, if we pause awhile and try to unravel a work as a whole, that we shall be amply repaid,—by meeting thoughts face to face, which are none the less real and valuable because it is some hundreds of years since they issued from the brain of the thinker.

Unfortunately many great series of paintings are completely destroyed; some are much defaced, and can only be seen in fragments; others again having been for various reasons covered with whitewash, on discovery, have been cruelly "restored." Of this last there is a glaring instance in one of the chapels in Santa Croce in Florence, where a figure in one of the Giotteschi frescoes has been painted in again with the addition of a *gens d'arme's* cocked hat.

But in spite of these many and various misfortunes, a considerable number of story series happily still remain, and can be examined in detail, and the thought of the artist in them deciphered and studied. Perhaps in its day Santa Croce, the head-quarters of the Franciscan Order in Florence, was as richly decorated as church could be, bare as it appears at the present time. In 1853 were discovered in its

ARTISTS AS STORY-TELLERS

eastern chapels some of Giotto's finest works, and it is believed that there still exists, awaiting to be released from its present coating of whitewash, a series of frescoes, running all along the nave, under the clerestory, illustrating the Divine Comedy. It is supposed that at the time of a visitation of the plague, the whole church was lime-washed, and the presence of these enrichments came, with the lapse of years, to be forgotten. At present, money is lacking to carry the discoveries further, which were begun in 1853. We may, however, even now see there a most interesting "Life of the Virgin" by Taddeo Gaddi, Giotto's favourite pupil, the above-mentioned frescoes by Giotto himself, illustrating the life of St. Francis, and scenes from the lives of Saints John the Baptist and the Evangelist, and also by Agnolo Gaddi, the story of the "Finding of the Cross."

To this task of story-telling the painters one and all addressed themselves, and according to their individual temperaments and genius was their dramatic success. We have seen how in this matter of dramatic truth Tiziano fell short, great painter though he was. Ghirlandajo again, a painter of great ability, gives us a long series in the choir of Santa Maria Novella, Florence, of the life of the Virgin, but to him also, the story, as a story, is of secondary importance; what he concerns himself with is rather picturesque grouping, the folds of his draperies, and the furniture of his rooms. It is to Giotto that we must turn, as to the prince of story-tellers; and when we are accustomed to what may at first appear quaint in his style, to our modern eyes, we feel his power. He has left us some magnificent series. In Padua is a little chapel, built in the centre of what is now an oval garden, and was once a Roman amphitheatre. Early in the fourteenth century this site was given to a certain knight, who having among his friends formed a society which they called the Brotherhood of the Virgin, utilised the materials here given him to build a chapel in the Virgin's honour. The Madonna dell' Arena, it came to be called. The walls and vaulting of this chapel Giotto received the commission to decorate with the story of the Life of the Virgin.

Here, then, with his family he removed that he might prosecute the work, and here also Dante found a resting-place at the same time; and tradition says that poet and artist together enjoyed each other's society, possibly each inspiring the other in his labour.

Contrary to the manner of the two painters last named, Giotto was never led away from the stories he had engaged to tell, by any desire to show how much more he could accomplish. The story of "Giotto's O" is intensely characteristic of the man.[1]

[1] The story referred to is that the Pope, having sent to Florence to seek out the most able artists to undertake some work he wished to prosecute in Rome, his ambassador called at the shop of Giotto to ask for specimens of his skill to show to his Holiness. Giotto, dipping a

Plate XVIII.

To face page 111.

St. Joachim in the Wilderness. Giotto.

From a photograph by Naya.

ARTISTS AS STORY-TELLERS

With the same master's hand which drew the O, he sweeps in his figures in grand simple lines, the whole pose indicating the spirit he wishes to express. In this Arena series, the painting representing St. Joachim retiring into the wilderness after having been repulsed at the altar by the high-priest is a masterpiece of expressive drawing (Illustration 18); every line of the simple folds of his drapery, as it falls from the bent figure, shows with the figure itself, the weight of depression that is on the good man's heart. Only two shepherds, a dog, and some sheep, and the most conventional rock background, represent the wilderness. The former greet him with rustic incomprehension of his profound feeling, and thus while falling into the story, set up no counter interest of their own to distract the attention from the principal event. As with this painting, so is it in a greater or less degree all through Giotto's work.

From Padua he was called to Assisi to decorate the great church there erected in honour of St. Francis. There always seems to have been a strong sympathy between this robust masterly painter and the gentle Francis; at any rate, the Order of Brothers Minor appear never to have wearied of giving him commissions, and though the painter allowed himself to give expression, in verse, to some disapproval of the

pencil into his colours, with one sweep of the hand drew a perfect circle, and handing that to the messenger, declined to send any further specimen of his ability. The Pope, hearing the tale, appreciated the metal of the man, and gave him his commission to execute.

Franciscan fantastic cult of poverty, no one painted the saint himself with tenderer touch, while the fresco in Assisi of the marriage of Francis with his Lady Poverty is one of the master's highest and most poetical efforts.

The church of Assisi is a double one, the lower a sort of glorified crypt, the upper one the church proper. In the upper church, along the south, west, and northern walls runs a series of frescoes illustrating the life of the saint from his early youth up to the miracles performed at his death. A quaint charm runs through the whole series, which shows, as it were, in a glass the lovable character of the hero of the romance. One seems, in following the story step by step, to bridge the centuries and to know the man, and almost to feel the magnetism of his personality. Truly a triumph this in the matter of story-telling. Another series we have still left to us, again painted for the Franciscans, and if not by Giotto, strongly under his influence, to adorn the sacristy of Santa Croce, but now preserved in the Florentine Academy. This, on small panels of wood, represents the life of Christ, and then again scenes from the life of St. Francis. In Ruskin's "Mornings in Florence" he draws the visitor's attention to two small frescoes, attributed to Giotto, in the first cloister of Santa Maria Novella, and with his sympathetic insight points out from this what we feel may well have been in the mind of the painter as he worked. In fact, perhaps nowhere could a better introduction to the spirit of Giotto be found than in the references to him and his work throughout the above-mentioned little volume, and the tract entitled "Giotto and His Works at Padua." To patiently follow our English master's guidance through these pages gives one for ever afterwards an insight into beauties which truly prove themselves to be a joy for ever.

Besides the series above mentioned as being in Santa Croce, by the two painters Gaddi, two other series in Florence may be mentioned. Running around the walls of the sacristy of the beautiful church of San Miniato al Monte is the story of St. Benedict, painted by Spinello Aretino, another of the Giotteschi. The tabernacle of Orcagna in the church of Or San Michele has a sculptured series of the life and death of the Virgin, but this monument is reserved for more detailed consideration later. The façade of the Duomo of Orvieto is another monument of sculptured story—the Creation, the Life of Christ and the Last Judgment are there illustrated; while Benedetto Majano's pulpit in Santa Croce, Florence, has in its panels scenes from the life of St. Francis. These, of course, are merely selected examples of a widely spread form of art work, and none of them, nor others of their like, can be fully appreciated without a knowledge of the story which they relate. The artist may appreciate their artistic excellences, the craftsman their technical qualities, but behind these elements lies the story, from one point of view the *raison d'être* of the whole, and which he who runs may read, or of little benefit to him will be his running.

If among the Italians Giotto may be said to have a rival as a teller of stories, we must look away out of Tuscany, and among the painters of Venice. There, unique among the magnificent assembly of Venetian masters, stands one who, though with them, can hardly be said to be of them. The very sound of his name, Vittore Carpaccio, seems to strike a note of the fantastic and the original. Little is known of his personal history: he is believed to have been born at Istria; he was already an artist in 1479, and was still alive in 1523. That he was capable of painting the serious balanced group, sacred in character and religious in aim, with majestic forms and splendid draperies, is abundantly shown by a "Presentation of Christ in the Temple," now preserved in the Venetian Academy; but even here his peculiar freshness of spirit seems, as it were, to bubble forth in a little figure seated at the feet of the saints who enter the Temple precincts with such serious dignity. Raphael himself could not be more tenderly delicate in his delineation of a child angel, and there is in addition a quaint grace in this small person who sits with knees crossed so as to support an all too large mandoline, which the Tuscan masters, in their intenseness, would never have conceived. There is in her no connection in

ARTISTS AS STORY-TELLERS

thought with the classic Cupid, which one must trace in even Raphael's "*putti*"; this little soul is Carpaccio's very own, and one of the sweetest little creatures of her degree in art. But when Carpaccio leaves the formal composition, and betakes himself to telling stories, then indeed the stream of his originality flows. He is not severely dramatic like Giotto, but a veritable romancer,—a kind of Hans Andersen among the painters,—he revels among fancies, quaintnesses, and delicate beauties, and withal maintains a thread of moralising throughout.

In Venice we have three great series of his,—the largest, in the Academy, is the story of St. Ursula ; and in San Giorgio degli Schiavoni, we have the legends of St. George and St. Antony.

This story of St. Ursula, with its wild romance, its flashes of truth to human nature, was just such a one as we may imagine would attract the mind of Carpaccio. So imbued with life and human nature is it in fact, that the tale has an intrinsic interest for us to-day, as well as for the mediæval worshipper of saints.

St. Ursula came to be reckoned as the patroness of the school-girl, of teachers of girls, and particularly of virtuous girlhood generally ; and thorough girl she is herself, in her fantastic story,—brilliant, quixotic, wilful, devoted, flashing through difficulties by sheer force of her bright personality, carrying most grave and reverend seniors off their common-sense feet by this same force, and its sweet directness; hers is a tale for all time, and Carpaccio the man of all others to be its illustrator.

The wife of Theonotus, the Christian King of Brittany, died,—so runs the story,—leaving behind her a little daughter, Ursula. Ursula was singularly gifted both in body and mind, and soon was able to fill her mother's place in the court, and as the counsellor of her father. She was, besides, very learned. She knew all that had happened in the world's history from the time of Adam downwards; she knew the name of every plant on earth, and star in heaven; and, moreover, she grew increasingly beautiful to look upon, and was a devout Christian. The report of her spread, and, crossing the Channel, reached the ears of Agrippinus, the heathen King of England; and Carpaccio opens his series with a representation of the coming of the ambassadors of Agrippinus to Theonotus, to ask the hand of Ursula in marriage for his only son, Prince Conon. King Theonotus, in the picture, sits under an embroidered canopy, by the side of a wide canal of the Venetian type, while buildings rise across the water, of Italian Renaissance architecture. Thus far, Venice is the world to our painter, as to his brethren in art. Theonotus, for the moment, can give no reply to this undesired demand. Behind the throne, however, is depicted a neat little bedroom, and there sits the King with all his perplexity written on his face, telling his fears to his daughter, who, standing before him, counts upon her fingers the pros and cons of the affair. Agrippina is too powerful to offend with impunity,—and yet he is a heathen; the King sees no way out of the difficulty. Not so Ursula; to her a plan brilliantly simple unfolds itself, and she persuades her father to adopt it. She will, she says, accept Prince Conon, but granted three conditions. First, for her must be apppointed in Britain ten noble virgins as maids of honour, and to each of these must be given one thousand attendants, and to herself another thousand, —eleven thousand in all. For three years must the marriage be deferred so that she may, while still a virgin, go on pilgrimage, and visit the chief shrines of the Saints; and lastly, Prince Conon himself must, before the marriage, be baptized. Either, thought she in her wisdom, these conditions will be deemed too hard, and on the other side will be the refusal, not ours; or, if I must give myself away, I win with the gift eleven thousand souls, and that of the Prince, from heathendom to holy Church. And so the ambassadors were sent away, having first seen the Princess. Their farewell audience, Carpaccio thinks, took place within doors, in a chamber of exquisite refinement and severity in its architecture and decoration. The elegant gentlemen of England make their bows, while a clerk, as dainty as any one of them, squares his elbows over a side-table, as he draws out a fair copy of the conditions.

That night—the night after her diplomatic activity, —Ursula had a vision. Carpaccio shows her to us in her bed (Illustration 19); the room is as dainty a young girl's bedroom as any 'sweet girl graduate' among us moderns could devise,—her books, her reading-table, are all there, her plants in the half-open window, her pet kitten lying asleep, and her little shoes, placed side by side, are on the floor by her bed, while at the foot, on its cushion, neatly rests her crown. She herself, most girlish and fresh, lies tucked up in her white and embroidered coverlets. But the door of the chamber is open, and entering is a heavenly messenger, bearing a palm-branch in his hand. It is the angel of the Annunciation of Death. Ursula will go her way, he tells her, and the end will be a glorious martyrdom.

Carpaccio next transports us to England, the wild savage country still unchristianised, to which, however, he gives a curiously Venetian aspect. Conon is represented as a princely figure enough, with long fair hair, and habiliments of quite the Venetian cut and beauty. The ambassadors detail the conditions, but at the same time bring such a report of the beauty and excellences of the Princess, that Prince Conon makes no difficulty about any item in the document. He was baptized, and then sent forth, east and west, to gather together the required eleven thousand virgins, and forthwith ships them across to Brittany. Ursula received them, and gathering them all together in a

Plate XIX.   To face page 118.

THE VISION OF ST. URSULA.   CARPACCIO.
From a photograph by Naya.

meadow, through which flowed a stream, she preached to them the doctrines of Christianity, and that with such a sweet persuasiveness that one and all became converted to the faith, and were baptized by her hand in the stream. And now, having accomplished so much of her great scheme, she sent for Conon, and Carpaccio, in a series of dainty groups, shows us the arrival of the Prince, his meeting with Ursula and her father, and, finally, the embarkation of the Princess with her attendants for Rome, which was the first place they wished to visit, in the three years of pilgrimage among the shrines of Christendom. Here Carpaccio bethinks him that, in the wild unchristianised England, he has done wrong to make life still smile along the banks of palace-bordered canals, and among Venetian architecture generally; so, though on that side of the picture which represents the court of Brittany he retains the Venetian style, the habitation of the English King, on the other side of the picture, he conceives this time as a structure of irregular Gothic. This, thinks he, is sufficient indication of savagery! While the virgin band embarked, Conon was left in Brittany to comfort his prospective father-in-law, Theonotus. As one would suppose, the intrepid maiden band refused all masculine help for their voyage; some say an angel, in each ship, took the helm; but be that as it may, with such wisdom and success was the fleet navigated, that in due time from their leaving Brittany for Rome, they arrived at the port of Cologne! Here again a heavenly revelation was accorded to Ursula, that this was the place where she would, later, receive her martyrdom, and not herself alone, but all those who were with her. This news she shared with her attendants, and they joined her in giving thanks to Heaven that they were counted worthy of so great an honour. They then set sail for Basle, and thence began the laborious journey over the Alps; but Heaven having brought them so far, again came to their aid, and angels were their guides and sustainers, until they reached the plains of Italy, —and so, at length, they arrived in Rome. Meanwhile Prince Conon could not content himself with the task his lady had appointed him, but in his impatience, had also set off for Rome, and, by miraculous aid, he arrived on the same day as Ursula and her eleven thousand made their entry.

Carpaccio shows this dual entry, and their meeting with the Pope Cyraicus. He, and a train of ecclesiastics, wind down from the direction of the castle of St. Angelo, and Conon and Ursula, with sweet youthful rapt faces, kneel side by side, to receive his benediction. Again Ursula triumphed for the faith, this time over and above her wildest hopes and dreams. Conon, so impressed with the religious atmosphere engendered in this field of meeting, begged to be baptized anew by the Pope's own hand, and took the name Ethereus to express the thorough regeneration of his soul; and further, to give practical proof thereof, he released

ARTISTS AS STORY-TELLERS

Ursula from her vow to him, determined to forego his marriage with her, but to join her as a brother, in her pilgrimage, and also in her expected martyrdom. The spirit of exaltation spread, and the Pope announced his intention to go with them, and also win the martyr's crown. Some more earthly-minded of the attendant ecclesiastics remonstrated with him, saying it was not fitting that an old man should go this wild journey, with so many maidens; but the Pope's pure enthusiasm was untouched by such unworthy considerations, and some bishops also joining, the band thus augmented, all embarked and set sail for Cologne.

Now Cologne at that time was being besieged by Huns, and some treacherous heathen captains resident in Rome, being aware of the voyage of this strange company, sent word overland to the King of the Huns, warning him of the expected visitation, for they feared that by the means of so many Christians, of such exalted faith, that the heathendom of all Germania would be threatened. But thus unwittingly, their action merely served to work out the Saint's plans and desires. Carpaccio next gives us the arrival of Ursula's ships at Cologne, and one sees the timid old Pope aboard, who now that the time has come, seems sadly to need fresh inspiration from his girl guide. He looks over the ship's side with the greatest anxiety, as do the bishops behind him, all in their mitres and robes. The soldiers about Cologne, at first appear wonder-struck at the sight of these numerous ships, and their strange crews, and one sees them running from out the gates to investigate, while only one, and he with the utmost leisure and nonchalance, bends his crossbow and places a bolt. However, in the next picture we see that the Huns remember the message they have had from Rome, and are determined to preserve their heathenry in spite of such a gallant attempt to wrest it from them. They have allowed the ship's companies to land, and are falling upon them. At first they killed off the men for the most part, and hoped to keep the women alive, but these resenting the consequent insults intended, and coveting the crown of martyrdom so dearly, wore out the patience of their enemies and gained their much-desired death,—all but Ursula. Awed by her majesty in this supreme moment, no one dared to touch her, and the king, struck by her marvellous beauty, on the instant offered her marriage. Indignantly she refused, and then defied him, so that his pride arose and he struck her down. Thus she too received the immortal crown. In the right of the picture, Carpaccio shows her being carried on a bier by some surviving bishops, to her burial,—her face, quiet and peaceful, lies uncovered, and over it is a soft glow as of sunset light, the ending of her day, an end that to the painter was full of glory.

In the last picture of all, curiously fantastic, he has almost overpassed the bounds of dignity, which

ARTISTS AS STORY-TELLERS 123

throughout the rest had been most delicately preserved. The apotheosis of St. Ursula is the subject. The martyr's palms of the eleven thousand virgins, won through her leading and example, are here gathered together in one green sheaf, and on it, as on a pedestal, the saint stands raised above her fellows, with eyes turned upwards to heaven, from which God the Father bends, with outstretched arms, to receive her. The eleven thousand kneel round, the tiara'd Pope among them, with their eyes fixed upon their girl saint.

Much less known generally than either Giotto or Carpaccio, and yet a great master of the form of art which we are now considering, was Duccio di Buoninsegna, almost the earliest of the masters of Siena, and a contemporary of Giotto. Of his labour comparatively little is left, but his principal work, a great altar-piece for the cathedral of his city, though deposed and cut into several pieces, may still be seen in the museum of the Duomo.

In the contract drawn up between Duccio and his employers he pledges himself to execute the commission "to his best ability, and as the Lord shall give him cunning," and to the fulfilment of his contract he bound himself by an oath on the Evangelists. He was three years engaged on the work, and when it was finished, it was, like Cimabue's better-known Madonna, carried in procession from his shop to the cathedral, preceded and followed by priests, the chief officers of the state, and a crowd of citizens, fasting and with lighted candles. The bells all rang and business was for the day suspended "in honour of so noble a picture"; and after it was placed in the Duomo "the rest of the day," says the chronicle, "was spent in prayer and almsgiving to the poor, beseeching God and His mother our advocate, to defend us from adversity and evil, and preserve us from the hands of all traitors and enemies to Siena." As we see it to-day, in the museum, it is shorn of all its original architectural setting; the paintings alone remain, but in them we can trace a beauty of sentiment, which makes us feel that the wording of his contract was no vain conventional phrasing, but simply and literally meant by the great painter. The altar-piece, as originally set up, was painted on the back as well as the front; the two parts are now divided, and hang side by side. On the front is a dignified group of saints and angels surrounding a throned Madonna. On the back is a series of twenty-six small compositions, illustrating scenes from the Passion and the Resurrection. Probably nowhere in art has the gospel story been followed, step by step, with such detail and such earnest attention to all that the artist deemed must have happened under the given circumstances; the old story is brought to life again, scene after scene, by Duccio's devout and sympathetic pencil.

By the side of this great "tavola" covered with

the twenty-six compositions is a number of detached panels, which may or may not have belonged to the altar-piece, in its original form, before it was displaced, and sawn asunder, to facilitate its removal. Some of these carry on the story of Christ after the resurrection, and others give the final scenes of the story of the Virgin.

In connection with the " Presentation of the Virgin " by Tiziano, the first part of this once popular story was related, and this will perhaps be a convenient point, in the prosecution of our subject, to continue the relation.

Mary, given up, and presented by her parents to the Lord, was duly received by the high-priest into the Temple, where she, as already stated, continued "day by day in all holiness, in prayer and meditation and the study of the word of God, holding converse with angels, and fed with celestial food from heaven, and increasing in stature and wisdom and grace before God and man," and that until she arrived at the age of fourteen years. Then the high-priest considered the time come for his charge to be betrothed, and being guided by a heavenly vision, he announced that only he whose rod budded would be considered worthy to espouse the marvellous maiden. A number of youths, of the sons of the priests, greatly desiring her, presented their rods accordingly to the high-priest, and he laid them all before the Lord in the Temple, but in the morning not one of the rods had budded. Much concerned, the priest sent to learn, if in any other place the will of the Lord had been made known. And there was found by his messengers one Joseph, an elderly man of the house of David, a widower, whose rod had budded, but he through humility had not revealed the fact. Joseph was then brought before the priest, and solemnly espoused to the Virgin Mary, to whom he became not so much a husband, as the guardian of her virginity. The other aspirants when they saw that their suit was hopeless, in their grief and disappointment, broke their rods and went their way.

This subject of the "Sposalizio," the high-priest joining the hands of Mary and Joseph, while the disappointed suitors break their rods, is one frequently depicted by Italian artists. The next great event in the Virgin's history is the annunciation, which being biblical it is unnecessary to repeat, and from this point the story of the Madonna merges into that of her Son until after the crucifixion. Then the devout again took up the thread of the narrative, and, who can say out of what substratum of truth, the following story was woven; and it is this latter part of the tale which Duccio has illustrated, with the same sympathy which he expended on the scenes from the Passion.

After the ascension of her Son into heaven, the tradition continues, Mary went as He had desired

ARTISTS AS STORY-TELLERS

her, to the house of John, the beloved disciple, beside Mount Zion, and there lived, honoured by all, until the age of sixty years. And at that time she was sitting in her house, earnestly thinking of her Son, and desiring to be again united to Him; and there came to her a second time the angel Gabriel, bearing, however, in his hand a branch of palm from Paradise, its leaves glittering like the morning star. And the angel bade her be comforted, for in three days she would have the desire of her heart, and be with her Son for ever. Then Mary, greatly rejoicing, prayed that two boons might be granted to her,—first, that her sons the apostles might be gathered around her when she passed away; and second, that in that last moment she might not see Satan. And Gabriel promised that these things should be. And Mary sat in her house waiting for the fulfilment of his word. Now, the apostles were dispersed in different parts of the earth, preaching the gospel, in obedience to the command. John was in Ephesus, and as he preached it thundered, and a cloud caught him up and bore him to his house beside Mount Zion; he entered, and Mary greeted him with joy, and told him what was about to befall. And, after John, came in the other apostles, all brought from their several labours by the power of Heaven. And John in his turn told them the great news, bidding them, however, not to weep, "since they who preach the resurrection must not give cause for it to be said that they fear death."

And being thus assembled, they all sat together waiting until the third day; and Mary having prepared her bed, lay down, and on the third day the room became filled with heavenly visitants, Jesus Himself among them. And he spoke to the soul of Mary, and it departed out of her body in the form of a little child, pure and white, and He received it into His arms and bore it up to heaven. Then certain women prepared her holy body for the grave, and a heavenly light shone round about it, and screened it from their sight, though their hands wrapped it in the grave-clothes. And when all was prepared, the apostles placed the body upon a bier, and Peter and Paul bore it, while John carried the heavenly palm before it. The others ranged themselves on either side, and so they carried it to a newly-made tomb in the valley of Jehoshaphat. And angels joined the procession, singing, "This is she who is beautiful among the daughters of Jerusalem, even as ye have seen her, full of grace and love." The apostles, too, sang a psalm as they walked, and a cloud came down and surrounded them, so that they could not be seen; only the sweet singing was heard. And all the city heard the song, and wondered greatly, and the Jews in wrath ran after the apostles, that they might seize and burn the body. And the high-priest placed his hand upon the bier, to stop its progress, but his hand withered so that he could not draw it to himself again, and all the people who were with him were stricken with blindness. But Peter touched with the heavenly palm those who confessed that Mary was the Mother of God, and they were healed. And so the Madonna was laid in the tomb, and the apostles watched by it for three days; and on the third day they saw the heavens open, and Christ upon His throne, and He sent down to the tomb of Mary, and by His power her body arose, and her soul, which had rested in His arms, joined her body, and both together rose up to heaven, and bowing before her Divine Son, Mary received a heavenly crown, and was seated by His side in His celestial glory. But Thomas was not with the apostles when these things befell, and when he heard the tale he could not believe, for it seemed to him to be too wonderful. So the brethren bade him come with them to the tomb, and see that it was empty, and he came and saw indeed that the holy body lay no longer there, but that the tomb was filled with blooming flowers, both lilies and roses; and as they stood around, they turned their gaze toward heaven, and again they saw beyond the sky, and on her throne the blessed Virgin, crowned. And she looked with kindness upon Thomas, and loosening her girdle, let it fall into his hand, which precious relic of

I

her compassion is preserved in the Cathedral of Prato, in Tuscany.

Almost every incident of this story is illustrated by Duccio, with unfailingly tender touch and sympathy. One cannot but marvel at the original genius of the man, who sprang at a bound, and unaided, from the bonds of Byzantine tradition into such gracious freedom and living art.

From Duccio to Raphael is a great leap, but though Raphael was a blossom of the full Renaissance, he, too, in common with the earliest masters, entered into the lists as a teller of stories.

A magnificent series designed by him, though executed for the most part by his pupils, may be seen in the Villa Farnesina, in Rome. In this case the frescoed series is in a private house, in what was probably once a gay reception room, when Renaissance Rome was at the point of its utmost brilliancy. The decorative scheme, in perfect harmony with the place and time, is taken from classic mythology, and illustrates the story of Cupid and Psyche. The ceiling has a curved surface, and it is upon this that the story is depicted. According to precedent, the action of the tale runs round the lower part, filling up the curve of the vaulting, while the consummation is reserved for two large compositions in the middle, on its comparatively flat expanse.

This story, one of the most beautiful in any

mythology,[1] Raphael has treated in a partial manner; the incidents which happened on earth, and connected with human beings, Psyche herself excepted, he has omitted. In this light, airy chamber, built for gay throngs of the beautiful Children of the Renaissance, one is transported out of this earth into Olympian regions, and only that part of the story is depicted which relates to classically divine persons, and their connection with the events of the myth. We see Cupid's joy in his discovery of so much beauty, and his mother's consequent distress. One is made to feel even a certain sympathy for the angry goddess as she brings her plaint before Jove, as who should say, "Am I not Beauty itself? where, then, is the reason of my being, if you permit a rival, and that an earth-born woman?"

Mercury, the messenger, flies so that one almost hears the quivering of his wings, as he obeys the command to seek the unhappy Psyche. Charming is the group of Cupid, in his turn pleading before the Olympian Grand-parent, who, quaintly enough, having given his thunder-bolt to his eagle to hold, crushes the wilful boy's cheeks in his hand as he kisses him, and promises that he, too, shall have his way. In the last of the series, Psyche ascends, guided by Mercury, her labours over, her joy within

---

[1] For the whole of this story, told in English as beautifully as can be well imagined, see vol. i. of W. Pater's "Marius the Epicurean." The original is in Apuleius.

reach, her rest before her,—all is expressed in her upward rapturous glance, and her composed limbs; and then the ceiling proper bursts forth into her reception among the assembled gods, and the marriage feast, with her restored divinity.

The whole is full of charm, and grace, and feeling,—worlds apart, however, from any of the other series mentioned above, since the didactic is entirely absent, and yet, for that reason perhaps, the more entirely characteristic of the crest of the Renaissance wave to which it belongs. Thus a note on it is demanded, in order to round fitly any survey of the subject of the Italian artists as Tellers of Stories.

CHAPTER V

THE COMPARATIVE TREATMENT OF SUBJECT

THE feeling of many a traveller unacquainted with the genesis of Italian art was probably expressed by the wearied American *nouveau riche*, who complained to a sympathetic companion :—

"Don't you think, sir, these Italian painters worked just rather too much in a rut?"

The remark was the result of correct observation, doubtless after visiting conscientiously all the galleries that lay in his route; and from his standpoint Italian art was certainly and unblushingly "in a rut." The same subjects are, in fact, endlessly repeated; originality of subject was evidently a matter about which the old Italians concerned themselves very little. They bestowed labour on their productions; thought, ingenuity, nay, the loftiest genius were expended in their art; but the greatest of them all still painted the same old tales and subjects. The Creation, the Madonna, the Christ, Tobias and the Angel—again and again we see them, and others of their family. Yet it is obvious that it was not that the artists could not be original in this matter of subject, but that they deliberately would not go out of their "rut." In fact our modern artists' method of seeking the world over, from East London to Japan, for new subjects and suggestions, and original themes, they probably would have laughed to scorn as unworthy of the dignity of Art.

The interests of the world were narrower in those days, but possibly they were proportionately deeper; and the artists concerned themselves with the deep things of life, with various aspects of the accepted religion of the day, or of the precious New Learning, that came to be counted hardly less important than religion. Then concerning the former class of subjects, the religious, these had an additional hold upon the artist, in that in their artistic form they were for the most part handed down through venerable tradition, which tradition was held to be most binding.

It must always be borne in mind that the birthplace of the highest forms of Christian art was Byzantium. In that city was early developed by Greek artists a purely Christian architecture, and with it a purely Christian style of ornament, conventional in form, and richly symbolical in spirit. As time passed on, at the close of the seventh century a council of the Church was held there, to discuss the question of religious teaching by means of art, and the conclusion come to was, that the churches

TREATMENT OF SUBJECT 135

should be enjoined to discontinue the exclusive use of symbols in ecclesiastical decoration, as a method of giving instruction, and, on the contrary, to encourage the direct representation of sacred things. As an immediate consequence of this decree of the council of Constantinople, within one century there sprang up a whole cycle of sacred compositions, which in time became traditional, and stamped with authority throughout almost all Christendom, as well in the West as in the East. That representation of the Trinity in Unity, for example, in which the crucifix is held in the hands of God the Father, while the dove hovers between the two, is one of these Byzantine compositions, handed down century after century, and treated with endless modifications by different artists, who always, however, preserved the essential elements. Besides compositions of this order, a series of historical scenes was selected, and not only the scenes themselves, but even their general arrangement and composition were preserved by tradition. So that even Michel Angelo and Raphael, when treating any one of these venerable subjects, painting with all their gigantic powers of execution and original thought, started in the first instance, not from their own unbiassed personal conception of the scene, but from a mountainous accumulation of tradition as to treatment and sentiment.

No fewer than twenty-four of the well-known sacred subjects illustrated in art, ranging from the

Creation to the Last Judgment, are enumerated by Lord Lindsay as belonging to this ancient Byzantine cycle. These, then, endeared by nearly a millennium of association, became almost consecrated by the same force. And still further, it must be remembered what position, quite apart from art, these subjects held in the mediæval mind. They were matters of vital importance, since they dealt with what were held to be God's most intimate dealings with mankind. Hence, no wonder they kept their hold, and were repeated in varying guise, acccording to the ability of the artist. He did not wish to change the subjects, any more than he wished to change the universe. In fact, to replace this cycle of subjects could only become possible by a universal change, since they represented to him the profoundest verities of existence. But in the treatment of them, to lavish all his skill, his power, his invention, his genius, that was his pride and joy. He did not wish to cease painting the Queen of Heaven, the Divine Mother, but, with his increasing powers, only to render her ever more regal, more universally maternal; and as with the Madonna, so with the rest.

One of these traditional subjects, the Creation, is among those above mentioned as sculptured on the façade af the Duomo of Orvieto, and there we may see a beginning of originality of treatment; a something of the artist's own, added over and above what the tradition demanded. The scenes are the Creation

Plate XX. To face page 137.

1 THE CREATION. CATHEDRAL OF ORVIETO.
From a photograph by Alinari.

TREATMENT OF SUBJECT

of Birds, of Beasts, of Man and Woman. These were what the artist had given to him to represent, as an artist, however, not as a slave. And to him came the vision of the Creation, when the Word went forth, such as had not occurred to the artists who had preceded him. Though in the beginning the earth was void, not so the universe, for according to mediæval belief a most regularly constituted system of Intelligences existed beforehand, of Angels, Archangels, Principalities, Powers, Virtues, Dominions, Thrones, Cherubim and Seraphim, these last nearest to God Himself. These, thought the artist apparently, must have witnessed the work of the new Creation; it is written, "The sons of God shouted for joy." So here came to the sculptor, with the poet's imagination, his opportunity for originality. The subject is so great a one in itself, he would care for no change there, but into his treatment of it he introduces his own fancy (Illustration 20). Following the Creative Word, as He passes from one phase of Creation to another, are two attendant angels, watching the act with reverent wonder. In sentiment and in composition, this is a great advance in the treatment of the subject, and as we may see in later examples, what is here an innovation becomes in its turn almost a tradition, to produce, under more skilful hands, even more beautiful results.

The creation of Eve, we find here, as in all early representations of the story, is told with great distinctness. There is no slurring over the literal facts, as told in the book of Genesis. Deliberately the Creator makes the incision in the side of the sleeping Adam. And in the next scene (Illustration 21), as distinctly the Woman rises actually and literally from his side,—rises up towards the Creator, obeying the motion of His hand. But further, here at Orvieto, the Man is represented again, lying asleep, one might almost say even more than asleep, deathly in his utter prostration, while the attendant angels no longer stand together behind their Lord, but have separated, and are in this last panel standing apart, one at the head and one at the feet of the body of the sleeping Man. A very literal representation of the story this, crude indeed, some might even say comic in its crudity, at first sight—at any rate, a childlike conception of a childlike age. So it may be, but from one point of view only; it will be necessary to go still a step farther into the mediæval mind before this work, and others of the same order, can be judged at all rightly.

For in trying to understand the spirit of the mediæval artist's treatment of his subject, there is another point to consider beyond that of the venerable tradition which surrounded it—a point of the utmost importance, and one perhaps, more than any other, ignored by persons only anxious to have a general work-a-day understanding of mediæval art. Perhaps the best way in which to plunge for the moment into the spirit of the time, with regard to this matter, is to

11. THE CREATION. THE CATHEDRAL OF ORVIETO.

From a photograph by Alinari.

TREATMENT OF SUBJECT

see the actual words of one of the leading thinkers of the period. Almost the greatest of these, and perhaps the most representative figure of mediævalism at its best, is the poet Dante. In his *Convito*, a book part prose, part verse, he writes as follows :—

"We should know that books (or doctrine) can be understood and ought to be explained in four principal senses. One is called *literal*, and this it is which goes no further than the letter, such as the simple narration of the thing of which you treat. The second is called *allegorical*, and this is the meaning hidden under the cloak of fables, and is a truth concealed beneath a fair fiction, as when Ovid says that Orpheus with his lute tamed wild beasts, and moved trees and rocks, which means that the wise man, with the instrument of his voice, softens and humbles cruel hearts, and moves at his will those who live neither for science nor for art, and those who, having no rational life whatever, are almost like stones. And how this hidden thing (the allegorical meaning) may be found by the wise, will be explained in the last book but one.[1] The theologians, however, take this meaning differently from the poets; but because I intend here to follow the method of the poets, I shall take the allegorical meaning according to their usage. The third sense in which a book ought to be explained is called *moral*, and this, readers

---

[1] Unfortunately this "last book but one" of the *Convito* was never written; the first four of the original plan were completed, after writing which Dante abandoned the work.

should carefully gather from all writing, for the benefit of themselves and their descendants; it is such we may gather from the Gospel, when Christ went up into the mountain to be transfigured, and of the twelve apostles took with him but three, which in the moral sense may be understood thus—that in most secret things we should have few companions. The fourth sense is called *anagogical* or mystical, that is beyond sense, and this is when a book is spiritually expounded, which, although a narrative in its literal sense, by the things signified refers to the supernal things of the eternal glory, as we may see in that psalm of the prophet, where he says that when Israel went out of Egypt, Judea became holy and free, which, although manifestly true according to the letter, is nevertheless true also in its spiritual meaning—that the soul, in forsaking its sins, becomes holy and free in its powers and functions. And in such demonstration the literal sense should always come first, as that whose meaning includes all the rest, and without which it would be impossible and irrational to understand the others, and above all would it be impossible with the allegorical. Because in everything which has an inside and an outside, it is impossible to get at the inside if we have not first got at the outside. Wherefore as in books, the literal sense is always the outside, it is impossible to get at the other senses, especially the allegorical, without first getting at the literal."

So wrote Dante, expressing, however, not merely

his own private views, but the scholarly opinion of his age. St. Thomas Aquinas, the greatest doctor among the schoolmen, went even further. Man expresses himself and his thought by means of speech ; God, however—so taught St. Thomas—not having human limitations, speaks not only by *words* but by *things*. Thus everything was held to have a hidden and allegorical meaning, as well as its open and literal one. History in particular, it was thought, must be thus understood, in order to perceive the Divine meaning, which it was the intention of God to have expressed by the actions of His creatures. The Bible was, *par excellence*, a book " written within and without "—an opinion, in fact, held by certain sections of the community to-day. Allegory thus wrapped around all mediæval thought, and was deemed a high order of thought—a means of approaching the Divine meaning and mind.

In the light of this idea, it will be seen that these quaint sculptures of Orvieto will repay a further and closer examination. The Creation of Woman was deemed by the mediæval theologian to be a profound allegory—a story written within and without. There was its literal truth, devoutly believed ; then looked at from within, it had the following hidden and symbolical meaning ;—Eve, drawn from the side of the sleeping first Adam, represented or typified to the devout mediæval Christian the birth of the Church from the wounds of Christ, the second

Adam, to whom thereafter she should be espoused, and become the universal mother. With this profound allegory underlying the literal, it is not to be wondered at that no incident in the story could be omitted or slurred over in its artistic presentation. So the Orvietan sculptor represents the Creator Himself making the wound in Adam's side; what theology is not here implied? The Woman rises from this wound, not by her own or any natural power, but through the impulse given by the Creative Word, the Second Person of the Trinity, and she turns not to any earthly spouse, but to the heavenly, as she rises into existence by His will. Again, the wounded Adam is represented below, lying as if dead, with the two angels in their altered positions, one now at the head, and one at the feet, waiting for the moment when he will rise up from his sleep. Is it too fanciful to read into this last composition a suggestion of the Resurrection morning? So, with a naïve art, the charm of which is doubled by a consideration of its allegorical significance, did this old sculptor do his work; but with others sometimes the allegory overpowered the art. In the Bargello in Florence hangs a little terra-cotta relief of this same subject, 'The Creation of Woman,' executed long after the pillars of Orvieto—one wonders, indeed, how at that time a nation of artists could have accepted it, so crude is it in its conception of the scene (Illustration 22). Adam lies asleep; Eve has risen from his

Plate XXII.

THE CREATION OF WOMAN. IN THE BARGELLO.

TREATMENT OF SUBJECT

opened side, but with both arms around her, the Creator seems to drag her upwards, towards Himself. How fraught, however, with meaning are these same actions—the upward motion of the woman, and the strong embrace of the Creator—when the allegorical sense of the subject is recognised! And the strength of allegory in the mediæval mind is surely indicated in the fact that at the date of its execution, well on in the middle of our period, a composition so crude was accepted at all.

From these crude efforts we now pass to work of more skilful hands, and in this connection Ghiberti's Creation panel on the Baptistery gates again demands attention (Illustration 17). As noted above, this is a continuous composition, combining five different scenes in one panel, but among the five the most beautiful is the group of the Creation of Woman. It is in fact, perhaps, the most entirely beautiful representation of this incident in all art. One sees here a great difference in every way, from the scenes as sculptured at Orvieto. The idea of the attendant angels, for example, is marvellously developed. The two meek wondering spirits who follow from phase to phase of the creation, are here multiplied into an angelic host, filling in gracious line the heavenly regions of the upper part of the panel. Their presence, however, we feel is to fulfil an æsthetic rather than a didactic purpose, and so all through the work one notes this change of spirit, which is the inevitable course of artistic development, in the nature of things. With the advance of art pure and simple, symbolism must decline in artistic representation, and even the interest of allegory must lessen its hold on the artist as the claims of art itself become more engrossing and imperative. When the artist's hand can express nearly all his thought, he discards the symbol as an unnecessary toy, and what cannot be expressed artistically by direct representation is deemed a subject unfit for art. So in this panel, the wounding of the side of Adam is omitted. From the æsthetic point of view this was a necessity; nothing, and no manner of treatment, could make that a beautiful subject for art; only the wealth of hidden meaning could justify its representation at all. Ghiberti, then, the artist, and not of set purpose the theologian as well, rejects it. With absolute grace and æsthetic propriety the woman rises up from behind the man, and what the work loses in allegory it gains in art; and it must be according to the spectator's temperament that he decides which is the greater and more absolute, the gain or the loss. But as art, how lovely is this work of Ghiberti's! all sweeping together in gracious line and harmonious grouping, melting into and standing out from the background, as the sentiment or the art of the composition require, while here and there one sees the pure form nakedly displayed, and all so excellently made. Beautiful is the whole work, but the scene of the Creation of

Plate XVIII.   To face page 145.

THE CREATION OF MAN.   MICHEL ANGELO.
From a photograph by Alinari.

TREATMENT OF SUBJECT

Woman may be taken as the culminating point in the treatment of that most difficult subject.

The most glorious representation of the Creation of Man was reserved for Michel Angelo to conceive and to execute. On the ceiling of the Sistine Chapel, in the Vatican, five different aspects of the creation are represented. That of woman occupies the central space, since of woman was born the Christ, but it is the creation of man which is the artist's supreme achievement, and it remains unrivalled. The subject is of course the old one, steeped in the tradition of the ages. Michel Angelo accepted that as did all others of his craft, but in face of Michel Angelo's conception of that old subject, who can clamour for more "originality"? Was ever anything more marvellously original, and all the more so because of the age-long traditions which lay behind it? (Illustration 23).

The composition is grouped into two great masses, almost diagonally opposite to each other—the man below, his form simply sublime in its naked perfection; the Creator above, in a swirling cloud of drapery and waving hair; and the two masses are brought together by the outstretched finger-tips of each, which all but touch. There is apparently no ancient symbolism here; there is no hidden meaning of accepted allegory. Michel Angelo had his own thought to express, yet, though devoid of understood symbolism, it is no realistic conception, but a dream-picture of

K

the highest order, steeped in suggestiveness, expressed by the most virile and unerring art. In the two masses, the two great elements of the universe, earth and heaven, lie apart,—but earth moves in its sleep of the unborn, for heaven is coming down to it; and, approached by the finger of God—the union is not complete—earth takes form and awakes into man. Above, behind the Creator, held in his other arm, living apparently as yet only in his thought and foreknowledge, lie the generations of the unborn, and woman looks out with shy wonder at the new-made Adam, almost with an air of prevision of all that the coming creation may mean to her and hers. Here the brain and art of the man, Michel Angelo himself, work out their subject with supreme originality. Buonarotti, the human poet among the artists, puts his own soul and thought into his work. What matter the antiquity of the subject? his conception of it is all his own.

Here we see most magnificently displayed the way in which the old artists viewed what the Philistine is apt to consider their limitations—their "rut" to wit. Standing where they did as regards their knowledge of the universe, "Who wants," they seem to say, "to perpetuate one's own finite thoughts and poor fancies, when we have given to us the acts and purposes of the Divine mind to unfold? But we tax all our powers to unfold these worthily, according as to every man is dealt the measure of genius, or to

THE CRUCIFIXION. P. PERUGINO.

From a photograph by Alinari.

TREATMENT OF SUBJECT

quote old Duccio of Siena, 'as the Lord shall give me cunning.'"

The most important of all the traditional subjects was naturally the Crucifixion. In representations of this scene there are two questions always to be settled before judging of their merits.

First, was the artist intending to depict a theological aspect of what he considered the culminating point in the scheme of the universe? Or, second, was he trying to draw a dramatic picture of an historical event which happened outside Jerusalem A.D. 34? As a rule, Tuscan artists, and those who worked under Tuscan influence, attempted the theological presentation. Fra Angelico's great "Crucifixion" in the Chapter-House of San Marco is a case in point. Il Beato was strongly tinged with the old Byzantine spirit, through the school of Siena, by which he must have been profoundly influenced, and the Sienese painters were as a whole contemplative rather than dramatic in their art. So, here, in this Crucifixion it is the theological aspect of the event which is essentially the one the painter had in mind. Representative figures of all periods and all degrees are grouped together, in the act of contemplation of the Divine death.

Another great Crucifixion of this order is Perugino's in the Chapter-House of the now disused Convent of Santa Maria Madelena dei Pazzi in Florence (Illustration 24). The work covers the whole

of one wall, and is divided by pilasters into three
compartments. The cross, with the kneeling Magdalen at its foot, occupies the central space, the
Madonna and St. Bernard are to the left, Sts.
John and Benedict to the right. It is perhaps Perugino's finest effort, and all his usual characteristics
are, in it, well exemplified. We have his pale clear
sky, with trees silhouetted against it, and his soft
Umbrian landscape running into the picture, all
executed with an ineffable grace and charm. With
this exquisite delicacy of treatment, a wonderful hush
is brought into the great fresco. Stiller and more
contemplative than even Fra Angelico's "Crucifixion"
is this of Perugino. The words "It is finished" seem
to give the keynote of the work—a quiet of sunset,
and the ending of the day, pervades the whole. The
upper part of the sky, in the painting, is bathed in an
evening glow, which softens away towards the horizon. The mountains are in a purple light, and the
sun and moon, one on either hand of the Christ, are
tenderly darkened. The figure of Christ Himself
can hardly be rivalled in quiet and dignity. There
is no convulsion of grief in the watchers; obviously
they understand the significance of the immortal
death, and look on with rapt adoration rather than
sorrow. The Madonna who stands by, we see, has
passed through suffering to the further phase of
knowledge, and would seem almost indifferent in the
quiet of her face, were it not that in the hands which

TREATMENT OF SUBJECT

have been tightly locked together, and are now only just relaxing, we see how great has been the maternal pain. St. John, young and beautiful, forgets all in his inward vision of the meaning of the event. The whole is as devotional as Il Beato's—a touch more human perhaps, in that the drawing is more finished, but though human in no way dramatic.

For a dramatic representation we must go elsewhere, not to Umbria, not even to Florence. In that city, where of all others humanity was found all-absorbing, shall we find the scene represented, not in its theological, but in its dramatic aspect. In Venice, and by the hand of Tintoretto, that titan even among Venetians, we have this representation.

In the Scuola di San Rocco, in an inner room, one wall is filled with Tintoretto's conception of the scene, and there one finds one's self in a different world indeed (Illustration 25). Even before the original, it takes some moments to accustom the eye to the crowds there depicted, and to gather into one the numerous elements which at first do not appear capable of resolving themselves into an ordered composition. But by degrees it grows clearer, and the thought guiding the whole makes itself apparent. In the centre is the Christ, and at the foot of the cross a pyramidal composition including the Madonna, the other sorrowing women, and St. John. To the left of these is one of the thieves, bound to the cross, which men are hauling up by ropes into position.

Still farther to the left is an officer in charge, then some gaily dressed and mounted daughters of Jerusalem; then Jerusalem itself in the background, and some sad-looking, wind-blown trees against a cloudy sky. Coming round thus in the composition to the central cross, we see behind it a passing traveller on his ass, pausing on his way to see what it is that is astir. Going farther towards the right is the third cross on the ground, and the group near it engaged in binding its sufferer upon it. To the extreme right is another group of officials, and before them a man digging the hole for the third cross, while crouching under a low wall to his left are two soldiers casting lots.

These are the elements of the picture, and for the most part the traditional elements of the subject; all these and more has this valorous master taken, and where another would have selected, he has massed them all together in one great composition. But how are they treated? certainly not theologically. This painter has determined to see things as they are, hence the presence of all the recorded elements; and having obtained his mental vision of that historic scene, he has set himself to realise it on his canvas with all the consummate art of which he was the master. He has not conventionalised the horrible facts to make an artistic presentation, and certainly he has not been mystical, nor merely suggestive, but having imagined out of his full sympathy the Real, from that he has selected, with all the keenness of perception his art-faculty gave him, those points which best would give a proportioned representation of the scene, and these he has painted.

The supremacy of the Central Figure, in all this crowd, is secured by having it the only one already on its cross. The moment chosen is that just before the other two are in their places. Christ is alone. The halo that surrounds Him, the one note of the supernatural in the whole, is dimmed in the painting to an ashen grey, for this is no time of outward glory, but is the hour of humiliation. As to his face, where most artists' hands have failed, "Who," says Tintoretto, with grand humility, "who shall depict that in its living reality in this supreme moment?" He therefore paints it bowed down so that it is hidden in its own shadow. But when he turns to the others of the company, Tintoretto looks as a brother man, and his vision is intensely human. He is no theologian, he conveys no doctrine, he does not so much contemplate, as live in the story; he enters into the heart of each person there present, and paints him and her, not as an adjunct merely to a divine scene, but as he feels that he and she individually must have felt, if present and acting, in his or her own proper person, in that event. The workman as a workman digs his hole, and one sees in his stolid action, that he but thinks about the depth which he should make it. The officers in charge look purely official, and there to carry out the law. The thief already bound, and being hoisted up on his cross, one can see in the painting, quivers in helpless agony, quiescent from dull, lonely hopelessness; the second thief, not yet bound, though thrown upon the ground, is full of life, and looks keenly around, just once more, before the agony begins; the group at the bottom shows all the human anguish of mother, disciple, friend. St. John, one almost hears, groans yet again, "Let me go that I may die with him." Tintoretto has entered into the very heart of each, and then "to him was given the cunning" to realise his idea on his canvas.

There is yet another point, a feature not traditional, but introduced by the painter—the traveller, namely, on his ass. As he pauses, the beast bends his head, and sees a choice morsel, to an ass's taste, lying on the ground before him; crisp and dry lie withered palm branches, and Mr. Ruskin suggests why the painter conceived them as there. Strewn fresh and green the previous Sunday, before the coming king, this day when that king is enthroned in earthly shame, they are withered and lie soiled, trodden into the ground by common unthinking feet. To the representation of the utter isolation of Christ, and the sense of being forsaken, this puts the crowning touch.

This masterpiece of Tintoretto's is one of the world's masterpieces. No more dramatic painting of this great historical scene has ever been conceived. The brutal realisms, which occur in Rubens's

TREATMENT OF SUBJECT 153

otherwise justly celebrated work, are shamed before this consummate art, at once so real and yet so ideal.

Another interesting cycle of subjects for examination and comparison will also be found in the "Cenacoli," many examples of which may be seen in Florence. The Cenacolo, or Last Supper, was a very favourite subject for representation in the Western Church. We have it in Duccio's series of the Passion, painted on the back of his great altarpiece for the Duomo of Siena, and here a primitive arrangement of the company is preserved. In it the disciples are seated on both sides of the table, before and behind it, which arrangement necessitates the table being very much out of drawing in order to show both rows of faces; those in the front, too, sit with heads turned to right or left, so that their profiles at least may be seen, also they have no haloes, for obviously had these been there, they would have looked like golden plates laid upon the tablecloth behind them. St. John is represented as asleep, with folded arms, leaning up against his Master. The position assigned to St. John in the Gospel seems always to have puzzled the old painters, who had apparently quite forgotten the ancient custom of reclining at table; so they generally interpret it in this method, of making the youth asleep, and therefore, leaning upon Christ. This arrangement of the disciples all around the table seems to have commended itself to several generations of the older artists. It may be seen in the series of paintings of the Life of Christ attributed to Giotto, and formerly in the sacristy of Santa Croce, and now in the Academy of Florence. But as time went on, the painters discarded it. The subject came to be considered as an appropriate one for the decoration of convent refectories. There, painted in fresco, the grand feature of the apartment, occupying generally the whole of one end wall, it was necessary for the composition to be more seriously studied. So finally, the generally adopted arrangement was that of a long table across the end of the room, as it might be a continuation of the actual refectory, while the disciples are seated behind the table and at the two ends, the front side being entirely unoccupied. Though sometimes, and with a certain effect, one figure was left still seated on this outer side, that of Judas alone, thus and very pointedly, the only one of the twelve without the Apostolic nimbus.

Ghirlandajo (1449–1494) painted the subject thus arranged, twice in Florence; once for the Franciscans in the convent of Ognisanti, and once for the Dominicans in San Marco. The superior claims of Fra Angelico, in the latter place, often cause the visitor to hurry past the Cenacolo of Ghirlandajo, and yet it is well worth examination (Illustration 26). There is the long table across the end of the room,

Plate XXVI.   To face page 154

THE CENACOLO AT SAN MARCO. GHIRLANDAJO.
From a photograph by Alinari.

TREATMENT OF SUBJECT

with Christ as the central figure, the others on either hand, except the lonely Judas on the outer side, with his hand raised to dip his bread into the dish. Ghirlandajo was eminently one of the goldsmith painters; the early influence of the *bottega* is clearly evinced in this work, enriched as it is with lettering decoratively introduced, and other skilful ornamentation, as well as in its architectural fitness as a whole. Birds also are made a considerable feature among the accessories in this Cenacolo, some flying outside, and seen through the open arches. Two, however, are more prominent, one at either side of the picture perched on the ledges of two open windows. So prominent, indeed, are these made, that one cannot but conclude some hidden meaning is intended. The birds are the peacock and the dove, and the same are introduced and with the same actions, respectively, in the artist's other Cenacolo at Ognisanti, confirming the idea that some symbolic meaning is intended. The peacock, in early Christian days, had a clear and accepted meaning, that of immortality; the dove we still preserve as the symbol of the Holy Ghost. In the fresco, the peacock is just on the point of going out of the window on one side, while at the opposite side the dove is entering. It can hardly then be without deliberate intention that Ghirlandajo introduces into his work representing this Last Supper of Jesus, the symbol of Life as retiring from the company, while as it goes, it looks back and towards the entering dove, surely suggesting and implying the words, "If I go not away, the Comforter will not come to you."

In the disused convent of Foligno, also in Florence, is another most beautiful "Cenacolo" (Illustration 27); it is obviously painted under Peruginesque influence, so many of the Umbrian master's characteristics are present. The dainty landscape background, rising into hills on either side, and slender trees silhouetted against the sky, strike the eye at once, and then one perceives over the whole that devotional quiet with which Perugino knew so well how to suffuse his work. So beautiful is this Cenacolo, that many have been unwilling to attribute it to any less person than Raphael himself, in his Florentine days, before he took up his residence in Rome. The delicate question of correct and of incorrect attribution, is, however, for careful and skilled criticism to decide; for the traveller remains a beautiful Cenacolo to enjoy, and that none the less for being uncertain as to its author. In it, the company sits behind, and at the ends of the long table, the same arrangement prevailing as in the works of Ghirlandajo referred to above; true to Umbrian tradition and use, no dramatic moment is chosen, but a sense of gentle benediction is thrown over the whole; even the discrowned Judas, alone seated in front of the table, only gazes out of the picture darkly and sadly, as he grasps the bag in his left hand. The other

Plate XXVII.

To face page 156.

THE CENACOLO OF SAN SALVI. ANDREA DEL SARTO.
From a photograph by Alinari.

disciples look appropriately, but nothing more ; there is no marked individuality about any of them ; the whole is a magnificent piece of decoration ; it is, so to speak, a piece of decorative sentiment, exquisite mediævalism, on a high level of execution. The newer humanistic element is quite absent, everything is chastened and quiet ; even the agony in the garden, which is prophetically represented in the distance of the background, does not disturb the hush ; it rather takes the whole still further from the real, and makes it more distinctly a contemplation, and less a representation, of the scene.

Very different from this is the "Cenacolo" of San Salvi, another disused Florentine monastery, some fifteen minutes' walk beyond the Porta alla Croce (Illustration 28). For an afternoon[1] spent in a pilgrimage to San Salvi, every one must feel well repaid.

Browning's "Men and Women" has made us familiar with another renowned painter, Andrea del Sarto, one of the last of the great Florentine artists. As one meets and recognises his paintings in one gallery and another, one feels confirmed in Browning's estimate of this man. The "faultless painter" degraded by an unworthy wife, we see the story written everywhere in his work ; the wife's pretty face haunts him, he seems never to rise beyond her, and whether he paints Madonna or saint, Lucrezia

---

[1] For this work, the best light is in the afternoon.

appears as the model, till one wearies of the faultless painting and her insipid prettiness. It is with surprise, then, that one sees in the "Cenacolo" of San Salvi, a work of noble virility, and knows it to be by the hand of Andrea del Sarto. "The only Last Supper," writes Dr. Burckhardt, "which can be even distantly compared with Leonardo." The subject naturally forbids the presence of a woman; Lucrezia therefore cannot blight the work, and Andrea, apparently in consequence, works as a free man.

From the Cenacolo di Foligno, to that of San Salvi, we leap at a bound, from the pietistic and contemplative, to the dramatic and the greatly humanistic. Decorative adjuncts are here reduced to a minimum. We have the table across the room, simple as truth, a background of plain panelling and three windows to fill the upper part of the arch, under which the fresco runs. Nothing is introduced to take away from the dramatic interest; there is not a shadow of a symbol; all, even Christ, are without the conventional halo. Judas sits with the rest. St. John's traditional attitude is discarded; he is awake and alert at his Master's side, and with the others has just heard the astounding statement, "One of you shall betray Me;" and according to the character of the man does each one hear it. "What, does He mean that one of *us* is capable of such baseness?" seems to be the thought of Thomas, as he rises in his place, his fingers pressed tightly upon the table, while Peter, next to him, questions himself and turning his gaze inwards, asks, "Can it be, could *I*, in an impulse so far forget, and fall?" John, boyish and eager, extends one hand towards his Master's on the table, and in blank amazement says, "Is it I?" while with a movement exquisitely conceived, Jesus places His hand upon the lad's, as if to say, "No, no, not thou, be sure of that." And so through all the rest, with perhaps one exception, Andrea gives to us each man's inner thought. Judas is wonderfully represented; he is in this instance placed at Christ's right hand, and as throughout this work, the expression is given largely by the hands; nervous and pallid, the right almost trembles, as it rests upon the table, while the other moves upwards towards his throat, in the instant's hesitation, before he, too, forces himself to say, "Is it I?"

With all the varying shades of passion, however, which are displayed, nowhere is there undue exaggeration, nor any strain after effect; all is masterly and restrained. It is only before Leonardo's great last supper in Milan, that one feels that this scene can be depicted in even more masterly fashion. With the composition of this every one is familiar, even the "Raphael cartoons" now at South Kensington, are not better known. Unfortunately, however, we know it for the most part from reproductions not taken from the original, but from copies, and so faded and defaced is that original, in the old refectory of Santa Maria delle Grazie, that only a shadow of its pristine greatness can be traced. Yet even before this shadow, we feel in the presence of a greatness of creation and insight that is almost superhuman. Leonardo's painting ruined, surpasses other men's perfect work; and higher than his achievement it would be hard to imagine.

It must be understood that the above-mentioned productions are only selections from a wide field; even in Florence alone are other Cenacoli of considerable interest, and at varying points along the scale of evolution, from the simplest conception, to the later and more profound of the humanistic works. For of all religious subjects, this perhaps gained the most from the introduction of the humanistic element. Nowhere in the story of Christ is the pathetic human side of the picture more clearly displayed, and therefore so much the less does it lend itself to the contemplative method, and the more to the dramatic method of presentation.

As a further study of the comparative treatment of subject, it may be well to consider not only the evolution of thought and art, as we have done in the case of the Creation and the Cenacoli, nor varying attitudes of mind, as in that of the Crucifixion, but also the characteristics which properly belong to the two arts respectively, of Painting and Sculpture.

The legend of St. George will give the desired

TREATMENT OF SUBJECT

examples. This was the subject of one of Carpaccio's greatest efforts; a statue of St. George is perhaps the *capo lavoro* of the great sculptor Donatello; and Andrea Mantegna has left an exquisite little painting of the saint as victor, the combat over, and the dragon slain. The story of St. George was one which strongly appealed to the mediæval imagination. He was *par excellence* the saint of chivalry, and England was not alone in selecting him for a national patron.

His story briefly is as follows. St. George was a young Roman tribune and Christian convert. Travelling one day alone, to join the army, he met by the way a beautiful maiden, richly clothed, but apparently in profound distress. He stopped, and asked the cause of her grief, and was told that she was on her way to her death. A dragon of terrible ferocity had for long ravaged the country, and demanded periodically the offering of a virgin to stay his further fury. The lot that day had fallen upon her, and, king's daughter though she was, she was going to suffer the sad fate of her predecessors. St. George begged her to wait, and allow him to meet the dragon in her place. She refused at first, but at length, borne down by his assurances of victory, gave way, and they awaited together the coming of the beast. When he came in sight, St. George rode to meet him, and attacked him with his spear; this breaking, he had recourse to his sword, and with that completely disabled him. He then dismounted, and, taking the girdle of the Princess, bound the dragon, and led him, shorn of his terrors, into the city. The people prepared to give their deliverer wealth untold in reward for his services, but he refused everything, only asking them to accept baptism at his hands. They listened to his preaching, and then willingly consented. Later, in a time of persecution, St. George being very steadfast in his adherence to the faith, suffered martyrdom. He thus became the type of Christian chivalry, the saint militant. But that was not all; the story was held to be one of those "written within and without," it had a most profound allegorical meaning. The combat of St. George with the dragon signified, allegorically, the struggle of the spiritual nature of man with his lower carnal nature—spirit against flesh. So, in representations of St. George, it must always be borne in mind what was the complete idea that the artist desired to represent in treating this subject.

In the church of San Giorgio degli Schiavoni may be seen Carpaccio's treatment of the story in three paintings, the first one of the series having perhaps the fullest inner significance. The whole series is in the painter's most fantastic style, exceeding in that particular even the series of St. Ursula, and being generally more finished and per-

Plate XXIX.

St. George.   Carpaccio.

TREATMENT OF SUBJECT

fect. In the chapter, "The Place of the Dragons," a supplement to Mr. Ruskin's "St. Mark's Rest," the writer, Mr. Anderson, very eloquently gives his idea, and the full symbolism of the first picture of the three (Illustration 29). More briefly worded, Mr. Anderson's interpretation is as follows. St. George is here represented as riding a brown horse, the colour of earth, and that which generally marks strength and endurance, for Carpaccio's idea is not that of an ascetic's victory, but of normal human nature disciplining itself to a life of temperance, and requiring all vital force to accomplish the task. The colour having this significance, the waving, billowy hair of mane and tail has a further suggestion that, though so amply endowed with vital force, there is over and above this strong physical life a kinship with the higher spiritual life. It is in accordance with the accepted symbolism of the time that the hair is made so prominent, it is in opposition to the horny spines of the loathly dragon, which in their turn were the type, also accepted, of depraved and bestialised existence. Hair, and the absence of it, according to Mr. Anderson, plays a great part in the symbolism of the whole. That of St. George is waving and tendril-like and full of life, while that of two victims half-devoured by the beast lies in heaps, matted together in a loathsome mass of corruption. " Near the coiled adder is planted a withered human head. The sinews and skin of the neck spread and clasp the ground in hideous mimicry of an old tree's knotted roots; the scalp is bare and withered—these things, though so painful, are made thus prominent as giving a key to a large part of its (the painting's) symbolism. Later Platonists, and among them those of the fifteenth century, developed a doctrine concerning the mystical meaning of hair. As a tree has its roots in the earth, and set thus must patiently abide, so man, being of other family . . . has his roots in heaven, and has the power of moving to and fro over the earth for service to the law of heaven, and as a sign of his free descent. Of these divine roots the hair is the visible type."

In every other detail of the work, similar symbolism may be discovered. The two ships are perhaps the most obvious in their meaning. One full sail and prosperous on the ocean of life, while the other has made shipwreck, having coasted too close to the rocks in the neighbourhood of the Dragon. The broken spear, too, has its inner meaning. In this, as in most representations of St. George, the final blow is with the sword—that of the Spirit—as needed in the conflict, over and above the strength of human wisdom, symbolised by the spear. The Princess, true to the old story, stands and watches her knight, but allegorically she represents the soul of man; the seven jewels of her coronet stand for the seven primary virtues, the central one of all, in the form of a cross, symbolising Faith. In the second picture, we see the Dragon in the city, bound by the girdle of the Princess, and led by St. George. It crouches to the ground, boneless and powerless; a wonderful contrast to the rampant beast which sprang out of its den to meet the saint, never dreaming of a superior power. It waits without a struggle the death-blow which St. George is about to give. The third painting of the series depicts the baptism of the King and Queen, and there, true to his quaint humour, Carpaccio sees to it that in pouring the water of baptism over the head of the King, he turns the vessel so that the stream may run from his head to the ground in front, and not on to his royal robes. Similarly, with his other hand, the careful saint holds his own robe well to one side.

Thus Carpaccio completes his series, and presents us with his St. George, and as a Painter has he done so,—with art, with fancy, rich colour, flowing line, and animated grouping; and, since the subject is didactic, he has steeped the whole in allegory and symbolism. To those who can read it, the work is closely written both within and without. His every inch is crowded with accessory meaning, helping out and supplementing the main action of the story. Saint, and horse, and Dragon, and Princess are there naturally, but also gruesome fragments of the dragon's victims, symbolic reptiles, ships, and what not, and the result is a wonderful picture, one we would not have altered, no, not by a line. It is a fantastic revelling in all that his art allows, which is entirely charming.

But put the subject into the hands of a Sculptor, and could it be treated thus? One feels at once that that would be impossible; all those qualities which so charm us in Carpaccio are just what are forbidden to great Sculpture by its very nature. In sharp contrast to the St. George of Carpaccio, then, is that of Donatello, now to be seen in the Bargello in Florence (Illustration 30). It is a single figure,—the treatment of the painter is all reversed,—instead of diffuse illustration, iteration and reiteration by principals, and accessory symbols, till there is no chance for the meaning to be lost, when once the key has been given, in Donatello's figure we have a reticent concentration. St. George stands alone; there is no dragon, no Princess, not even the broken spear to tell the tale,—a little panel in relief, placed in the pedestal below the statue, does that in a semi-pictorial way. The figure above is not set to tell the story, but to show us St. George himself, the personality which made the story possible. According to the nature of things, in great sculpture it is impossible to be pictorial; that, the materials of the art do not allow. The moment that is attempted we have as a result the dolls, the waxwork realisms of the modern Italian stone-carvers, who, by their very cleverness of hand, reduce their art to an absurdity.

Plate XXX. To face page 166.

ST. GEORGE.   DONATELLO.
From a photograph by Alinari.

TREATMENT OF SUBJECT

Donatello, on the contrary, reaches almost the loftiest plane of great Sculpture in his St. George. It is the spirit of the conception, the mediæval ideal of the militant saint and temperate manhood, which he has set himself to make visible. It is St. George himself, and not anything about St. George, which he would realise. So every line of the composition is drawn in harmony with that idea, strong, restrained, and at one with all the rest. St. George stands firmly on his two feet, his shield in front of him rests quietly on the ground, and against his knee; he makes no aggressive action, he merely stands ready, with no exaggeration whatever in his pose,—all is simple and calm, and yet in every line alive. The young Michel Angelo, it is said, gazing one day on this work, with a sculptor's appreciation of the masterly success of this quiet yet vigorous pose, exclaimed impulsively, " March !" Yes, he lives, or rather the idea he represents lives in him, for he is not, as it were, man made stone —that is the modern Italian sculptors' ideal in art —he is rather stone made man. The stone has taken the form of the master's thought, and so stands in lasting repose, a perfect work, not of imitation, but of art.

In these two examples given of the treatment of St. George, we may see the qualities proper to the two arts of Painting and Sculpture, carried almost to their farthest limits, each uninfluenced by the other. Carpaccio's work is pictorial in every way; he was a Venetian, and as a Venetian conceived his ideas in colour, and a wealth of figures and architectural elements, grouped and balanced into a beautiful harmony.

In Donatello's work we have great sculpture,—intense, reticent to the last degree, with no superfluous line of mere fantasy, but each and all absolutely needed to express the artist's thought,—that grand line, pure form, and profundity of method, which is proper to the highest form of the art.[1]

In a previous chapter attention was drawn to the great difference between the art of Florence and that of Venice, in that while the Florentine Sculptors and Painters worked hand-in-hand, developing their respective branches of art side by side, in Venice the painters went alone along their own rich way, almost entirely separated from all sculptural principles. Carpaccio's St. George is a case strongly in point. In the Venetian Academy, however, is preserved a little "St. George" by Andrea Mantegna, which shows very clearly, in the treatment of the same subject, what modification painting undergoes when disciplined by a recognition of the laws of sculpture.

In speaking above of the enthusiasm for all things classic, mention was made of the school where Andrea Mantegna received his training as an artist,—that opened by Squarcione, on his return to Padua, from

[1] A fine cast of this work is to be seen in the South Kensington Museum.

Plate XXXI. To face page 31.

ST. GEORGE. MANTEGNA.

Greece, with a valuable collection of antique sculptures. Padua was also rich in sculpture of its own. Donatello had received numerous commissions from that city, and some of his finest achievements are to be seen there in the church of San Antonio—bronze reliefs of simply marvellous execution and delicacy. Thus the surroundings of the young Mantegna were rich in examples of the severer art, and his works generally show how strongly he was influenced by them. Bearing in mind the special characteristics of Carpaccio's treatment of St. George on the one hand, and Donatello's treatment on the other, it is interesting to compare with them the St. George of Mantegna (Illustration 31). He stands in his oblong panel, almost as a statue in his niche, and yet he is not sculpture coloured ; Mantegna's work is true painting, but with a certain severity, a restraint in the lines, and a harmonising of them with the complete composition, which is essentially sculpturesque—and this gives a sense of satisfaction to the whole which it is hard to analyse, but which is, none the less, very present and actual.

In making the present selection of subjects from the "rut" of the *nouveau riche*, or, to speak more precisely, from the traditional cycle of sacred subjects, what is intended is to be suggestive rather than exhaustive. But it is hoped that the foregoing may be sufficient to indicate in what manner other and similar subjects may be viewed, so that they may appear not a monotonous repetition, but, on the contrary, a continuous variety, and full of interest, each one showing to a greater or less degree the mind of the artist who executed the work.

Such were the subjects of art in these centuries, otherwise that art would have been an anachronism; but the *manner* of the treatment was always a personal matter. Tradition helped the feeble, but never impeded the strong,—rather, standing on the fruits of tradition and past effort, the latter went on from these, into the realms of a sublime originality which produced from time to time such crowning glories as Michel Angelo's "Creation of Man," and Donatello's statue of St. George.

And now to conclude—let us sum up those considerations which, in the scheme of these pages, have been thought the most helpful in entering upon the subject of Italian Art.

It must always be borne in mind that in Italy, despite disasters, barbarian invasions, change of religion, and all the series of events which happened in the peninsula, from the fourth to the eleventh centuries,—deep down, trampled into the very soil, were the traditions of ancient Rome—traditions of civic life and municipal action, and these made the cities rise again after their fall, and, in rising, revert to Roman ideas of building, both as to construction and design. Though hands had grown clumsy, yet to this old style taste was wedded, and it was this that ever modified the newer influences, and determined the primary form of early Italian buildings. Byzantium might send her artists, and France and Germany theirs; the barbarian settlers might in their turn become builders; but underlying even their efforts, and transfusing all the rest, is the Latin element, the basis throughout.

Rome, however, could only teach what Rome herself had known,—and the Imperial City had, with all her grandeur, never been superlatively delicate in her workmanship. When building was well on its way to a great revival in young Italy, there arose the necessity for the more delicate arts of Painting and Sculpture—and then from the land of the ancient Etruscans rose that race of artists, who transformed the grim Basilicas into fairy lands of loveliness, with delicate fancies and exquisite workmanship. The hand of the goldsmith turned to Sculpture and Painting, his mind directed by the theologians through the maze of mediæval Christianity, produced an art which makes an epoch in the history of the human race. Thus came about that peculiar character which we recognise throughout Italian Art.

Then, putting ourselves further into the mind of the mediæval Italian, we may understand how it was that he painted and sculptured the things he did, and not another order of subject. One great function of art being to reveal the ideal which cannot otherwise be expressed, and mediæval ideals being what they were, it was these the mediæval artist depicted, and these one must realise in order to appreciate his art. Yet, as with us, these ideals were a continually shifting scene. Through the course of the three centuries under consideration, thought was modified, grew and changed, and with it, art, which developed by shades into new forms, each new form helped forward by the accumulation of what had gone before. These broad lines of consideration run through all Italian Art, and these must be realised first, and then, as time allows, or inclination urges, one may go further and appreciate the delicate differences between school and school, man and man, the interweaving of influence with influence, event with character, until each object of this lovely creation becomes in our ˙eyes a palpitating living thought.

Thus may be seen wherein lies the perennial interest of any national art, and that not alone for the students of art, but for all persons of intelligence. By means of it we are enabled to project ourselves into the mind of the age which produced it.

For it must be remembered that a great national art does not speak merely the thought of the elect few. To be national, it must speak, in the highest terms, that which is the common product of the time. What the people think vaguely and mutely, the artist thinks clearly and articulately. When his finished work is seen, they carry it in procession, as it were, and make holiday before it, recognising in it their own sentiment

TREATMENT OF SUBJECT

which they had not been able of themselves to express. "This is what *we* would do, if we could," they feel. That "if" alone marks them off from the artist—he is the one among them who *can*.

So the people feel; the artists take that inchoate feeling and give it form, the same, but idealised. The people see and recognise this idealised form, assimilate it, and giving off from that fresh thought, urge on the artists to higher flights. And so working together, the people and their artists, each helping forward the other, they build up a national art.

Thus the intimate thought, the very heart itself of a past age, is laid bare before us by means of its Art.

FURTHER NOTES FOR TRAVELLERS

I

A Florentine Masterpiece

It soon becomes apparent to the traveller that of all the cities of Italy where art flourished, Florence was the chief, the veritable metropolis from which flowed directly or indirectly to almost every other centre, knowledge and inspiration. And at the present time, despite spoliation, time, and the modern museum, there is still an almost inexhaustible store of art treasures to be found there. Among these is one monument supremely characteristic of the older Christian Florence, as distinguished from the later Florence, influenced by the New Learning; and as such, it will be perhaps useful as a supplement to the more general considerations in the body of this short study, to consider this particular work in some detail.

The monument referred to is the "Tabernacle" of Andrea Orcagna, in the Church of Or San Michele, which was spoken of in the first chapter. The exterior of this Church is a perfect school of the later sculpture, and standing prominently in the street, it cannot be passed by unnoticed. The interior is,

A FLORENTINE MASTERPIECE

however, much less well known. Almost square, it is divided into what may be termed a double nave. At the end of one of these divisions is the high altar; in the other and farther "nave," gleaming in its pure whiteness out of the gloom, which surrounds it as with a veil, to screen it from any mere careless gaze, is the Tabernacle (Illustration 4). Raised only one step from the ground, its topmost feature almost touches the vaulting. Roughly speaking, it is square in plan, with the angles elaborated into more complex form. The step on which it rests is surrounded by a marble and bronze railing, at each corner of which is a column surmounted by the figure of an angel. The lower part of the monument proper is occupied by a series of reliefs running in a course all around it, with a group of five smaller reliefs of single half-length figures at the corners. At the back, above this course, is a large panel in relief, and in the corresponding space in front is a painting, to enshrine which the Tabernacle was built. Framing all these, and surmounting the reliefs, a network of pure marble rises, spiral columns, gables, pinnacles, and sculptured figures, in convenient spaces lapis-lazuli, coloured marbles, enamels and mosaics are introduced; the whole being a marvel of design and workmanship. Orcagna has proved himself great as an architect, for the scheme as a whole is as great as the detail; the sculpture, his own hands' work, subsides into its place with infinite harmony, each part lovely in itself, and yet no part obtruding unduly, to take away from the general effect. Truly Florentine, *form* is supreme throughout. First the general design maintains its due supremacy, and then each detail down to the delicate cockle-shell ornament which surrounds the panels, is finished with the goldsmith's delicacy of hand and eye. Supremely beautiful it would be as *form* alone, and only as an enrichment of the already almost perfect form is the colour added. The richness of the material is absolutely secondary throughout. In fact the quality of that material is only valued because to it more delicate workmanship can be applied: thus it is richness without vulgarity, permitted only on account of intrinsic merit. The sentiment of the work is naturally religious, appealing to the current faith of the day. So that, taken as a whole, this Tabernacle is as perfect an example of the noble spirit of the older Florence as could well be found.

The story of its building is also characteristic. A certain early painter, Daddi by name, painted a Madonna which was hung up against a pillar in an open loggia in the city, where was a corn-market. This picture had not long held its place in the market, before it came to have attributed to it miraculous powers. In consequence, it was thought that it ought to be treated with an increase of reverence. Accordingly the outer arches of the loggia were walled in, and the once open market was thus transformed into an oratory, the name given to it being Or San Michele. In connection with the new oratory, a charitable society or company was formed in honour of the picture, called the company of the Madonna of Or San Michele. Some years later, in 1348, occurred a terrible visitation of the plague in Florence; gifts were vowed to this miraculous picture, both during the terror of the sickness and afterwards, as thank-offerings, when the plague was stayed, the final amount of these offerings coming to no less than 300,000 florins. The captains of the company then determined to devote a part of this immense sum to the building of a tabernacle to enshrine the painting, which seems not to have lost its reputation, despite the fury of the plague. The commission for this work was given to Andrea Orcagna, and he was told, in the grand Florentine manner, that it was to exceed all others in magnificence. His idea of magnificence has been noted above, literally greatness of workmanship, to which was added a greatness of thought equally characteristic of the mediæval artist.

As Wagner, in the modern art of music, could not away with a feeble libretto of questionable taste, to which to unite his great creations of sound, so when these older artists, in their older methods of art, went forth to create, they united their form and their colour to schemes of thought which were worthy to be so immortalised.

Orcagna's tabernacle was primarily a shrine for a picture of the Madonna. The name Madonna, however, to Andrea called up a very different idea from the one suggested to the Protestant mind of the North. To Orcagna, Mary, the maiden of Judea, was not merely an historical character of great interest, nor even was she only the heroine of a sacred romance, culminating in a heavenly throne, by the side of her Divine Son. Over and above all this, the Madonna had become to the devout mediæval Christian the perfect ideal of one half of humanity. As the human Christ was the perfect Man, so the glorified Madonna was the perfect Woman. This, then, was the theme of his work, the libretto so to speak of his form-creation, and that the above was his mental attitude, the finished work shows with the utmost clearness.

First, round the lower part of the monument are reliefs, showing selected scenes from the life of the Madonna. These are :—

1. Her Birth.
2. Her Dedication.
3. Her Marriage.
4. The Annunciation.
5. The Nativity.
6. The Epiphany.
7. The Purification.
8. Annunciation of her death.
9. The Death and Assumption of the Virgin.

The first eight of these panels are ranged round the base of the monument, two on each side, Nos. 1 and 2 on the north, 3 and 4 on the west, 5 and 6 on the south, 7 and 8 on the east side ; these last surmounted by No. 9. This is a large panel filling the space at the back, corresponding to that filled by the miracle-working picture in the front. These nine scenes represent the principal events of the Madonna's life, and in these it is to be supposed her character would be demonstrated, and how in all she fulfils the Christian ideal. Now this ideal, it was thought, may be expressed categorically by certain fundamental virtues, the sum of which makes up the perfect whole. First are the four cardinal virtues, Justice, Fortitude, Temperance, and Prudence; and next are the three theological virtues, Faith, Hope, and Charity. All these, then, are introduced into the scheme of decoration, and interwoven with the scenes of the Madonna's life.

The four cardinal virtues, represented by half-length figures in relief, occupy the principal place at the four corners, and, in addition, on either hand of each cardinal virtue, is the figure of another virtue of kindred significance, derived from the primary or cardinal one, and these are in turn each flanked by the figure of an apostle, thus making at the angles a group of five. The three theological virtues are placed on the north, west, and south sides between the reliefs, the corresponding place at the back, or east side, being occupied by a small door.

The virtues derived from the cardinal virtues are as follows. From Justice, come Obedience and Devotion; from Fortitude, come Patience and Perseverance; from Temperance, Humility and Virginity; from Prudence, Docility and Caution. Thus, beginning from the panel of the Nativity of the Virgin, the series runs as follows:—

North Side.
 The Birth of the Virgin.
 Faith.
 Dedication in the Temple.

North-West Angle.
 Apostle. Obedience. Justice. Devotion.
 Apostle.

West Side.
 Marriage of the Virgin.
 Hope.
 The Annunciation.

South-West Angle.
 Apostle. Patience. Fortitude. Perseverance.
 Apostle.

South Side.
 The Nativity.
 Charity.
 The Epiphany.

South-East Angle.
 Apostle. Humility. Temperance. Virginity.
 Apostle.

East Side.
 Purification.
 Door.
 Annunciation of Death.

South-West Angle.
 Apostle. Docility. Prudence. Caution.
 Apostle.

The connection of all these with the Madonna is worked out more or less fully as follows :—

First we have on the north side the virtue of Faith; on either hand are the Birth and the Dedication. Remembering the story of Saints Joachim and Anna, it will be seen how a fervour of parental faith in the revelation accorded them enwrapped the birth and early years of their child's life. Next to these comes Justice, with its derivatives, Obedience and Devotion, and following Devotion comes the Sposalizio. Obedience thus, as derived from Justice, comes next to the Dedication in the Temple, when the holy child submitted herself to the direction of the high-priest; while Devotion, the other derivative of Justice, comes next to the Sposalizio, or Marriage. The connection of thought is here very plain and happy. The panel next to the Sposalizio is the Annunciation, while Hope is between the two; this is obviously appropriate. Fortitude, with Patience and Perseverance, follow, with Patience next to the 'Handmaid of the Lord' hearing the Annunciation, and Perseverance next to the Birth of Christ. Here, too, the thought is connected. Between the Nativity and the Adoration of the Kings comes Charity—the Madonna is the channel through which flowed the divine love that sent the only-begotten Son to the whole world, to Gentile kings as well as to the chosen people. The next angle gives us Temperance, with Humility and Virginity; Humility, next to the Three Kings, Virginity, coming round to the east side, and next to the Purification. The next, and last, angle gives us Prudence, with Docility and Caution; Docility next to the Annunciation of Death, while Caution, being on the turn of the angle, comes, with less appropriateness, next to the first panel, representing the Birth of the Madonna.

Taken, however, as a whole, there is an exquisite continuity of thought running through the work, decorating the Madonna-theme with infinite suggestion, showing how all through the course of this chosen life, from birth to death, it was overshadowed by, or transfused with, all that goes to make humanity perfect. It must not be supposed, however, that this particular classification of virtues is all Orcagna's own; this, most probably, is derived from the patristic or the scholastic literature studied in his day; but the sympathetic art of the arrangement and choice of these, and the interweaving of them with the main theme, may safely be attributed to the artist, and herein lies the charm of this aspect of the work. But apart from this, which may be called the literary aspect of the monument, and greater than this, is its sculptural and architectural merit. Despite a certain quaintness of execution, the composition of each panel is most beautiful, the Sposalizio and the Epiphany specially so. In the former there is an exquisite grace, unsurpassed

A FLORENTINE MASTERPIECE 183

by Raphael himself, in his treatment of the same subject.

The figures of the Virtues are admirable, some having the greatest charm, and all, strong character. Sometimes the traditional attributes are attached, as, for example, to Justice is given the sword and scales; while again, in other cases, Andrea thought out his own symbol, or, of two traditional ones, chose the more subtle; in that of Temperance he has evidently done so. Generally this Virtue is represented as holding a cup from which she does not drink. Andrea, with a clearer insight, and wider perception of the realm of Temperance, represents her with a pair of compasses in her hand, with which to measure and divide, and find the mean. All these reliefs, as well as numerous statuettes which adorn the higher positions of the monument, it is said Andrea sculptured himself, while the details and accessories were wrought by assistants, under his eye and direction. It was a labour of ten years, and when its parts were completed, they were for the most part put together without cement, but block is held to block by clamps of metal with admirable results, for it still stands one of the most perfect and completed works of mediæval Florence. As such it is regarded by all who become imbued with the spirit of the old city, though so often it is passed unobserved by the cursory visitor. Yet were it desired to see in one single work all the principal characteristics and tendencies of this earlier period of Florence, perhaps no other monument in the city could better serve that purpose. It is preeminently fitted to unfold to a sympathetic observer the mind of that mediæval centre of intellectual activity in the moments of its highest inspiration and most masterly achievement, as another great sculptural monument, Michel Angelo's tomb of the Medicis, also in Florence, speaks more loudly than any other single work the later mind of the full Renaissance, that mind which is essentially modern. Orcagna's is the joyous, triumphant, completed art of the age of Faith; Michel Angelo's is the sadder art of the Age of Reason, oppressed by problems it has learned to ask, but never as yet to answer.

II

MEMORIAL RELIEFS

One of the interesting features of Tuscan churches, and very characteristic of them, is a certain style of memorial slab, inlaid in the pavement after the manner of our Northern Gothic " Brasses." Occasionally these are of bronze—one such, a very beautiful example by Donatello, may be seen in the north transept of the Duomo of Siena. For the most part, however, they are in marble, and in all cases the effigies are not incised as with us, but carved in low relief. With a most extraordinary lavishness these stones are laid in the church floors, and in any position, regardless of the innumerable feet which cannot but in the course of the years walk over them. As a consequence, by far the greater number are by this time almost trodden out of existence, faces are worn flat and featureless, and only the most important lines of the figures and draperies are left. In many of these, however, defaced as they are, may be seen traces of masterly skill and a most refined art, those few lines which are left being firm and graceful, and worked with an exquisite precision and delicacy of arrangement.

Yet, for the most part, the sculptors of those slabs are unknown. Evidently they were humble craftsmen whose names were not considered worthy of record; which fact presumably indicates the high standard of taste and workmanship common in their time. Santa Croce in Florence is very rich in these stones, and over two of them Mr. Ruskin has caused probably most English visitors to bend and recognise, or try to recognise, their excellences, worn away as they are to almost the barest outline.

In another church, however, outside the walls, the Certosa di Val d'Ema, three such slabs have been fortunately preserved in all their pristine beauty, so that it may be judged how much, and what quality of beauty has been literally trampled out of existence in numberless other instances. These three are really of extreme loveliness; one representing a young man in armour is especially so. He lies with his head leaning a little to one side in a pose of perfect rest. His armour is covered with the richest ornament, all worked in the stone in delicate relief, such as is rarely to be seen from any hand short of Donatello's. The other two, less elaborately worked, are hardly less beautiful in their general lines. These then, which by good fortune have been preserved to our day in almost perfect condition, may serve as an index to the full former beauty of many others which can now only be seen in outline, and as such are well worth a visit. In going over the Certosa, care should be taken, then, not to miss the lower chapel where these stones are to be found, and which, if not asked for, might easily be omitted in making the tour of the establishment.

INDEX

NOTE.—Names printed in SMALL CAPITALS are those of Persons.
" " " lowercase type " " " Places.
" " " *italics* " " " **Artists' Works.**

ALEXANDER VI., Pope, 44
Altar-front of Florentine Baptistery, 28
Altar-piece of Duomo of Siena, 124
ANDERSON, MR., 163
ANGELICO, FRA, 50 *et seq.*, 66
Annunciation by F. Angelico, 55
'*Arca*' of S. Dominic, 29
Assisi, 111-112
Assumption of Virgin, by Raphael, 78
Aurora, *The*, by Michel Angelo, 47

BARTOLOMMEO, FRA, 64, 81
BELLINI, GIOVANNI, 89
BENEDETTO DA MAJANO, 31, 113
Birth of Venus, by Botticelli, 41
Bologna, 21, 29
BOTTICELLI, 33-44
BROWNING, R., 34, 159
Byzantium, 14, 19; Council of, **134**

CARPACCIO, VITTORE, 114, 162
Cenacolo, by Duccio, 153; by Ghirlandajo, 154; school of Perugino, 156; by del Sarto, 157
Certosa di Val d'Ema, 185
COLVIN, SIDNEY, 43
Coronation of Virgin, by Lippi, **34**
Creation of Man, by M. Angelo, **145**
Creation of Woman, Orvieto, 137; Bargello, 142; Gates of Baptistery, 143; Sistine Chapel, 145
Crucifixion, by F. Angelico, 54; Perugino, 147; Tintoretto, 149

DADDI, 176
DANTE, 52, 56, 81, 110, 139

Dispute of Sacrament, 79
DONATELLO, 64, 90, 166, 184
DUCCIO DI BUONINSEGNA, 123, **153**

Etruria and ETRUSCANS, 24

Feast in House of Levi, by Veronese, 97
Fiesole, 50
FILIPPO LIPPI, 34 *et seq.*
Finding of Cross, by A. Gaddi, 109
Florence, 21, 23, and throughout
Foligno, Convent of, 156
Foligno, Madonna of, 82
Fortitude, **by** Botticelli, 36

GADDI, A., 109
GADDI, T., 109
GHIBERTI, S., 63, 64, 90, 104, 143
GHIRLANDAJO, 109, 154
GIOTTO, 73, 109, 110 *et seq.*

Hell, by Angelico, 57; by Signorelli, 69
Hospitality, by Angelico, 53

JULIUS II., Pope, 79

Last Judgment, by Fra Angelico, **56**; Signorelli, **68**
Life of St. Francis, by Giotto, 112; Florentine Academy, 112; by Benedetto da Majano, 113
Life of Virgin, by T. Gaddi, 109; by Ghirlandajo, 109; by Giotto, 110; by Orcagna, 113; by Duccio 125

INDEX

LOMBARDS, 20
Lucca, 16, 23

Madonna del Arena, 110
Madonna da Foligno, 82
Madonna of House of Pesaro, 95
Madonna of Or San Michele, 176
Madonna of Two Trees, 89
Magnificat, The, 39, 89
MANTEGNA, ANDREA, 63, 168
Mars and Venus, 42
MICHEL ANGELO, 30, 47, 105, 145, 167, 184
MORRIS, WM., 87

National Gallery, 11, 42, 45, 51, 97
Nativity, The, 42, 45
NICCOLA PISANO, 23, 29
NICCOLÒ DELL' ARCA, 30

ORCAGNA, ANDREA, 30, 113, 170
Or San Michele, 30, 113, 170
Orvieto, 51, 58, 59, 113, 136, 141

Padua, 63, 110, 169
Paradise, by Angelico, 58; Signorelli, 70, 73
PERUGINO, PIETRO, 74
Pisa, 22, 23
Pistoja, 23
PLATO, 32, 62
Prato, 130
Presentation of Christ in Temple, 114
Presentation of Virgin to Temple, 91
Pulpit of Santa Croce, 31

RAPHAEL, 72 *et seq.*, 130
Resurrection, The, by Perugino, 75
RUSKIN, 37, 112, 152, 185

S. Antonio, 169
S. AUGUSTINE, 107

S. Benedict, 113
S. Clara, 88
S. Croce, 31, 108, 185
S. Francis, 88, 96, 111
S. Frediano, 16, 21
S. Gemignano, 21
S. George, 115, 161 *et seq.*
S. Giorgio degli Schiavoni, 115, 161
S. Giovanni Laterano, 19
S. Marco, in Florence, 50, 154
S. Marco, in Venice, 19
S. Maria Madelena dei Pazzi, 147
S. Maria Maggiore, 18
S. Miniato al Monte, 17, 113
S. Pietro di Cassinensi, 19
S. Salvi, 157
S. THOMAS AQUINAS, 141
S. Ursula, 115
S. Zeno, 20
SARTO, ANDREA DEL, 157
SAVONAROLA, 40, 44, 81
Scuola di San Rocco, 149
Siena, 23, 123, 153
SIGNORELLI, 58, 65 *et seq.*
Silence, by Fra Angelico, 53
SPINELLO ARETINO, 113
Spring, by Botticelli, 41
SQUARCIONE, 63, 168 *f.*

Tabernacle, by Orcagna, 30, 113, 174 *et seq.*
TINTORETTO, 99, 149
TIZIANO OR TITIAN, 90 *et seq.*
Transfiguration, Raphael's, 83

Vatican, 75, 79, 84
Venice, 19, 85 *et seq.*
VERONESE, PAOLO, 97
Villa Farnesina, 130
VIVARINI, 88

WAGNER, 177

Printed by BALLANTYNE, HANSON & Co.
Edinburgh & London

Books Published by George Redway

BOOKS FOR COLLECTORS

RARE BOOKS AND THEIR PRICES. With Chapters on Pictures, Pottery, Porcelain, and Postage Stamps. By W. ROBERTS. 5s. net.

THE COIN COLLECTOR. By W. CAREW HAZLITT. With 12 Plates, depicting 129 Rare Pieces. 7s. 6d. net. *The Collector Series.*

FINE PRINTS. By FREDERICK WEDMORE. With 12 Plates. 7s. 6d. net. *The Collector Series.*

THE STAMP COLLECTOR. By W. J. HARDY, F.S.A., and E. D. BACON. Plates. 7s. 6d. net. *The Collector Series.*

OLD VIOLINS. New Volume of *The Collector Series.* By the Rev. H. R. HAWEIS. Plates. 7s. 6d. net.

THE CONNOISSEUR: Essays on the Romantic and Picturesque Associations of Art and Artists. By FREDERICK S. ROBINSON. 7s. 6d. net.

CANDIDE; or, All for the Best. A New Translation from the French of Voltaire, with Introduction and Notes by WALTER JERROLD, and 62 Vignettes and an Etched Frontispiece by ADRIEN MOREAU. £1 net.

THE GNOSTICS AND THEIR REMAINS: Ancient and Mediæval. By C. W. KING, M.A. Woodcuts and Plates. Second Edition. Royal 8vo, 10s. 6d. net.

THE TEMPEST. A Reduced Facsimile of the Play from the First Folio Edition of 1623, and the Modern Text of CHARLES KNIGHT on opposite pages. With Introduction by Dr. F. J. FURNIVALL, and Facsimiles of the Portrait by Droeshout and of the Original Music. With Glossarial Index, &c. Pott folio, art canvas, bevelled boards, 6s. net.

A WORD FOR THE NAVY. By ALGERNON CHARLES SWINBURNE. 1s. net.

THE WAYS OF THE WORLD. Vers de Société. By COSFORD DICK. 3s. 6d. net.

BEWICK'S SELECT FABLES of Æsop and Others. In Three Parts. To which are prefixed the Life of Æsop, and an Essay upon Fable by OLIVER GOLDSMITH. Faithfully reprinted from the rare Newcastle Edition, published by T. Saint in 1784. With the Original Wood Engravings by THOMAS BEWICK, and an Illustrated Preface by EDWIN PEARSON. 3s. 6d. net.

DICKENS AND HIS ILLUSTRATORS. By F. G. KITTON, Author of "Dickensiana," "Charles Dickens by Pen and Pencil," &c. With Portraits, Facsimiles of Original Sketches, &c. £2, 2s. net.

OLD PRINTS. By J. H. SLATER. 3s. 6d. net.

BIOGRAPHY

THE REMINISCENCES OF MISS M. BETHAM EDWARDS. One Volume. 15s. net.

FOUR GENERATIONS OF A LITERARY FAMILY. The Hazlitts in England, Ireland, and America. Their Friends and their Fortunes, 1725–1896. By W. CAREW HAZLITT. With Portraits reproduced from Miniatures by JOHN HAZLITT. In Two Volumes. £1, 11s. 6d. net.

THE SOLDIER IN BATTLE; or, Life in the Ranks of the Army of the Potomac. By FRANK WILKESON, a Survivor of Grant's Last Campaign. 2s. 6d.

EIGHTY YEARS AGO; or, The Recollections of an Old Army Doctor. His Adventures on the Field of Quatre Bras and Waterloo, and during the Occupation of Paris in 1815. By the late Dr. GIBNEY, of Cheltenham. Edited by his son, Major R. D. GIBNEY. 5s. net.

THE GREAT SECRET, AND ITS UNFOLDMENT IN OCCULTISM. A Record of Forty Years' Experience in the Modern Mystery By a Church of England Clergyman. 5s.

ANNA KINGSFORD: Her Life, Letters, Diary, and Work. By her Collaborator, EDWARD MAITLAND. Illustrated with Portraits, Views, and Facsimiles. Two Volumes. £1, 11s. 6d. net.

THE SECRET SOCIETIES OF ALL AGES AND COUNTRIES. A Comprehensive Account of upwards of One Hundred and Sixty Secret Organisations—Religious, Political, and Social —from the most Remote Ages down to the Present Time. By W. C. HECKETHORN. New Edition, thoroughly revised and greatly enlarged. Two Volumes. £1, 11s. 6d. net.

THE EARLY DAYS OF THE NINETEENTH CENTURY IN ENGLAND. 1800–1820. By WILLIAM CONNOR SYDNEY. In Two Volumes. (About) £1, 5s. net.

GREAT TEACHERS. Biographical and Critical Studies on Ruskin, Carlyle, Shelley, Burns, Coleridge, Tennyson, Emerson, Browning. By JOSEPH FORSTER. 5s. net.

DEVIL-WORSHIP IN FRANCE; or, The Question of Lucifer. A Record of Things Seen and Heard in Secret Societies according to the Evidence of Initiates. By ARTHUR EDWARD WAITE. 5s. net.

JAMES HAIN FRISWELL. The Story of his Life written by his Daughter, LAURA HAIN FRISWELL. 10s. 6d. net.

THE MEMOIRS OF THE LATE JOHN HERAUD. Edited by EDITH HERAUD. 10s. 6d. net.

MYSTICISM

NOTES ON THE MARGINS. Being Suggestions of Thought and Enquiry. Five Essays by CLIFFORD HARRISON. 5s. net.

THE GIFT OF THE SPIRIT. A Selection from the Essays of Prentice Nulford. Reprinted from The White Cross Library. With an Introduction by ARTHUR EDWARD WAITE. 3s. 6d. net.

HANDBOOKS

HOW TO WRITE FICTION, especially the Art of Short Story Writing. A Practical Study of Technique. 3s. 6d. net.

HOW TO PUBLISH A BOOK, or an Article, and how to Produce a Play. By LEOPOLD WAGNER. 3s. 6d. net.

THE ACTOR'S ART. Theatrical Reminiscences, Methods of Study, and Advice to Aspirants. Specially contributed by Leading Actors of the Day. Edited by J. A. HAMMERTON. Prefatory Note by Sir HENRY IRVING. 6s. net.

COMMON AILMENTS AND THEIR CURES. By Dr. ANDREW WILSON. 1s. net.

THE SYMBOLISMS OF HERALDRY; or, A Treatise on the Meanings and Derivations of Armorial Bearings. By W. CECIL WADE. 2s. 6d. net.

A DICTIONARY OF ENGLISH AUTHORS, Biographical and Bibliographical. Being a Compendious Account of the Lives and Writings of 700 British Writers, from the year 1400 to the Present Time. By R. FARQUHARSON SHARP, of the British Museum. 7s. 6d. net.

SPORT

CURIOSITIES OF BIRD LIFE. An Account of the Sexual Adornments, Wonderful Displays, Strange Sounds, Sweet Songs, Curious Nests, Protective and Recognitory Habits of Birds. By CHARLES DIXON. 7s. 6d. net.

TRAVEL AND BIG GAME. By PERCY SELOUS. With Two Chapters by H. A. BRYDEN. With 6 Original Drawings by CHARLES WHYMPER. 8vo. 10s. 6d. net.

GREAT SCOT THE CHASER, and other Sporting Stories. By G. G. With Portrait of the Author. 3s. 6d. net.

ANIMAL EPISODES, and Studies in Sensation. By G. H. POWELL. 3s. 6d. net.

SPORTING SOCIETY; or, Sporting Chat and Sporting Memories. Stories and Wrinkles of the Field and the Racecourse; Anecdotes of the Stable and the Kennel; with numerous Practical Notes on Shooting and Fishing. Edited by FOX RUSSELL. Illustrations by RANDOLPH CALDECOTT. Two Volumes. 12s. net.

COMMON SENSE IN CHESS. By EMMANUEL LASKER. 2s. 6d. net.

NEW SPORTING STORIES. By G. G. 3s. 6d. net.

IN SCARLET AND SILK. Recollections of Hunting and Steeplechase Riding. By FOX RUSSELL. With Two Drawings in Colour by FINCH MASON. 5s.

THE CHASE. By WILLIAM SOMERVILLE. Reprinted from the Original Edition of 1735. With a Memoir of the Author. Illustrations by HUGH THOMSON. 5s. net.

FICTION

THE BEAUTIES OF MARIE CORELLI. Selected and Arranged, with the Author's permission, by ANNIE MACKAY. 2s. 6d. net.

A TRAGEDY OF GRUB STREET, and Other Stories. By S. T. ADAIR FITZGERALD. 3s. 6d. net.

DAVID DIMSDALE, M.D. A Story of Past and Future. By MAURICE H. HERVEY. 3s. 6d. net.

BEYOND ATONEMENT. A Story of London Life. By A. ST. JOHN ADCOCK. 4s. 6d. net.

THE LURE OF FAME. By CLIVE HOLLAND, Author of "My Japanese Wife." 3s. 6d. net.

THE OLD ECSTASIES. A Story of To-Day. By GASPARD TREHERNE. 3s. 6d. net.

A HUSBAND'S ORDEAL; or, The Confessions of Gerald Brownson, late of Coora-Coora, Queensland. By PERCY RUSSELL. 3s. 6d. net.

THE TANTALUS TOUR. The Story of a Theatrical Venture. Chronicled by WALTER PARKE, Joint-Author of "Les Manteaux Noirs," and other Comic Operas. With Illustrations by J. HARRISON. 2s. 6d. net.

A BRIDE'S EXPERIMENT. A Story of Australian Bush Life. By CHARLES J. MANSFORD, Author of "Shafts from an Eastern Quiver," &c., and JOHN A. INGLEBRIGHT. 3s. 6d. net.

ROSALIND; or, The Story of Three Parrots. By E. M. HARRIS. With Frontispiece by E. D'AVIGDOR. 3s. 6d. net.

A DARN ON A BLUE STOCKING. A Story of To-Day. By G. G. CHATTERTON. 2s. 6d. net.

ELLIE AND THE CHINA LADY. A Tibetan Fairy Tale. By SIBYL HEELEY. 2s. net.

TOBACCO TALK AND SMOKER'S GOSSIP. Anonymous. Cloth, 1s. 6d. net; paper, 1s. net.

TO BE READ AT DUSK, and other Stories, Sketches, and Esssays. By CHARLES DICKENS. Now first collected. 6s. net.

9 HART STREET, BLOOMSBURY, LONDON

www.ingramcontent.com/pod-product-compliance
Lightning Source LLC
Chambersburg PA
CBHW031728230426
43669CB00007B/282